CONTENTS

PART I. CAMPS AND CAMPING

Chapter I. Preparing to Go Camping
What camping really means. Choosing campmates. Camping outfits. Clothing. Provisions.

Chapter II. How and Where to Camp
Where to camp. Selecting a camp site. What to look for. The best camp to use. Building a lean-to. Shacks. Tepees. Tents. Permanent camps. Canoe camps. Gypsying by auto.

Chapter III. Camp Housekeeping   .
Building fires. Fires without matches. Woods and their properties. Useful plants and trees. Camp cookery. Camp furnishings. Making beds. Handy hints to campers.

PART II. TRAILING AND TRAMPING

Chapter IV. Trailing and Tramping
Packing. Trails. Blazing a way. Direction and distance. Getting lost. Signs and signals. General woodcraft. Training ear and eye.

Chapter V. Emergency Hints   .   .
Accidents, Drowning. First Aid. Bandaging. Poisons and antidotes. Insect and snake bites.

PUBLISHER'S NOTE

Want to reconnect with nature and spend more time in the woods?

Have we got the products for you!

Just kidding. But also, kind of not. Like everything else in modern society, our relationship with the wild world has been put through the wringer of what cultural critic Anne Helen Petersen calls "the sinkhole of optimization culture." Want to go camping? Obviously, you need a tent. But not just any tent, you need to find the best one: ideally the tent with the best reviews, at the perfect price point, and with the weight, size, and color that best fits your trip, budget, and personality.

And it's not just the tent: you need the perfect sleeping bag, sleeping pad, backpack, camping stove, dehydrated meals, water filter. Not to mention picking the destination. At least, if you're not so exhausted by your research that you opt to spend the weekend indoors scrolling on your phone instead.

Take as a remedy this book originally published in 1917 as *The Book of Camping* by Alpheus Hyatt Verrill. Verrill lays out a list of items to bring, but instead of spilling ink on how to choose the "best" type of camping, he jumps right into what he sees as the most important choice: choosing the right camping companions. Only after that does he invite you to carefully consider your packing list, and goes on to offer extensive guides to the skills he thinks you'll need, from tracking to cookery to first aid. He's fiercely opinionated about

HOW TO SURVIVE IN THE WOODS

Camping, Fires, Trailing, Tramping, Getting Lost, and Finding Your Way Home
© A. Hyatt Verrill

9781648413643
This is Microcosm #283
This edition © Microcosm Publishing, 2023, 2026
For a catalog, write or visit:
Microcosm Publishing
2752 N Williams Ave.
Portland, OR 97227

All the news that's fit to print at www.Microcosm.Pub/Newsletter.

Get more copies of this book at *www.Microcosm.Pub/HowSurviveWoods*

Find more & How to Make It work at *www.Microcosm.Pub/HowToMakeIt*

To join the ranks of high-class stores that feature Microcosm titles, talk to your rep: In the U.S. **COMO** (Atlantic), **ABRAHAM** (Midwest), **BOB BARNETT** (Texas, Oklahoma, Louisiana), **IMPRINT** (Pacific), **TURNAROUND** (Europe), **UTP/MANDA** (Canada), **NEWSOUTH** (Australia/New Zealand), **APD** in Asia, Africa, India, South America, and other countries, or **FAIRE** in the gift trade.

Did you know that you can buy our books directly from us at sliding scale rates? Support a small, independent publisher and pay less than Amazon's price at **www.Microcosm.Pub**

Global labor conditions are bad, and our roots in industrial Cleveland in the 70s and 80s made us appreciate the need to treat workers right. Therefore, our books are MADE IN THE USA.

EU Safety Information: https://microcosmpublishing.com/gpsr

Microcosm Publishing is Portland's most diversified publishing house and distributor with a focus on the colorful, authentic, and empowering. Our books and zines have put your power in your hands since 1996, equipping readers to make positive changes in their lives and in the world around them. Microcosm emphasizes skill-building, showing hidden histories, and fostering creativity through challenging conventional publishing wisdom with books and bookettes about DIY skills, food, bicycling, gender, self-care, and social justice. What was once a distro and record label started by Joe Biel in a drafty bedroom was determined to be *Publishers Weekly*'s fastest-growing publisher of 2022 and has become among the oldest independent publishing houses in Portland, OR, and Cleveland, OH. We are a politically moderate, centrist publisher in a world that has inched to the right for the past 80 years.

what type of axe you bring, but believes you don't even need a tent—a tarp and some rope will do, maybe a piece of mosquito netting.

Of course, in this author's lifetime, ultralight-weight tents weren't available; if they were, you might have found him holding forth about the best make and model around the campfire (which he wouldn't have needed a match to start). You may decide you'd like to journey back in time and camp exactly as he advises in this book, but we suspect it's more likely that you'll take the tools, advice, and reminders that suit your needs and enjoy contemplating the rest from the comfort of your cozy nest of modern materials, knowing that if some disaster strikes, you'll be better prepared than before.

Critical thinking and making your own choices are key to both surviving in the woods and reading this book. While colorful and competent, this book is full of reminders of why its author might not be the ideal camping companion for the modern reader. A friend and contemporary of Theodore Roosevelt, he was an "explorer," zoologist, inventor, artist, and prodigious writer of popular science and science fiction. Verrill traveled the world and wrote about the people he met, but it's clear that at least as of this writing, he had not taken the opportunity to reflect with humility on his prejudices about them. He wrote this book implicitly for a young, able-bodied, white male reader of his time. We've chosen to republish this work so today's readers can take what they need. Just as we are not editing out the author's insistence that the second-most important piece of gear for any camper is a good axe, we are also including his most objectionable language and perspectives intact. This is to avoid hiding or protecting his legacy from scrutiny, and so we don't forget the cultural norms and assumptions of just a century ago. It's also because we trust you, today's reader, to know your own mind and think through everything you read in forming your own opinions.

If you read only one book about camping, you'll have one person's strong opinions about camping. As a teenager (coincidentally, growing up, like Verrill, in New Haven, Connecticut), I read as many camping and backpacking books as I could get my hands on. Once I achieved my goal—the Appalachian Trail—I immediately found that the reality in the woods was far different than what any of those books described. I had prepared myself for a solitary wilderness survival trip and was delighted to find myself in a haphazard linear sort of party instead. I needed very different skills to survive the highly social atmosphere than what I'd prepared for. Instead of basking in the perfection of my thoroughly-researched plans, I learned the key lessons of surviving in the woods: improvisation, openness to learn and work hard, and—a lesson that still holds true a century later—the importance of choosing my traveling companions wisely and being a good campmate myself.

Elly Blue

Portland, OR

July 2025

CHAPTER I

PREPARING TO GO CAMPING

THE term "camping out" covers a multitude of meanings. To many, life anywhere in the open is "camping out," and so-called "camps" are often commodious, comfortable, modern houses with electric lights, running water and all modern conveniences and are merely dubbed "camps" because they are built in the woods or away from settlements. Many people speak of "camping out" for the summer when they dwell in a flimsy tent on the beach or near the water at some crowded summer resort, while still others rent a shack or a farm house and purchase their supplies at the village store, and delude themselves into thinking they have "camped" for the summer.

But none of these methods of spending a few weeks or months is really camping out in the true sense of the term. To really camp one should be beyond the reach of motor cars and dance music, beyond sight of fashionable clothes and crowded summer resorts, and far enough from civilisation to make one more or less dependent upon the resources of nature and one's own skill and knowledge of woodcraft.

To be sure, camping out under such conditions necessitates a certain amount of discomfort and perhaps some hardships, but to overcome these, to make oneself a home and to provide all the necessities of life by one's own efforts and skill— in this lies the real enjoyment of camping out.

In order to do this, however, the camper must know something of woodcraft, must select his camping place and his camp with intelligence and must choose his or her camp-mates with care, for a poorly selected camp site may spoil all one's pleasure, grumbling or lazy companions are worse than none at all and a camp must be provided which is as comfortable and secure in foul weather as in fair.

There are many kinds of camps, each adapted to some special purpose, certain conditions and surroundings, or which possesses certain advantages.

There is a vast difference between camps for a permanent residence of several weeks or months and camps erected merely as shelters for the night, and before deciding what camp to use, what supplies you will require or where you are to camp, you should look into the matter thoroughly, determine where and how long you are going to camp and learn all you can of the surroundings, character and resources of the country you are to invade.

You can go camping in boat, in canoe, in carriage or by automobile, or you can pack your belongings on your back and tramp, pitching your tent or making your primitive home wherever night finds you or humour invites you to stop and tarry.

We often hear some one state that a certain type of camp is the best, but as a matter of fact there is no "best" camp. Tents, tepees, lean-tos, log and slab houses, shacks, wattled and thatched huts, even caves and dugouts, have their uses, and each can be used to best advantage only under certain definite conditions and for certain purposes. Sometimes several different kinds of camps may be used on a single camping trip, especially if one-night camps are made and the campers travel by boat, canoe or motor car. In a densely wooded country far from the settlements, log houses, lean-tos or similar camps may prove the best and easiest to make; in a district where timber is scarce, or where one is not permitted to fell trees, tents, tepees or other portable shelters are often advisable, and in places where there is no timber these are necessary. But to carry tents or portable camps is very difficult even with a canoe or other means of transportation, and the space which such a portable camp occupies may usually be used to greater advantage for other commodities, unless, as already mentioned, it is impossible to provide other means of shelter.

CHOOSING CAMPMATES

But even before deciding upon the type of camp you will use, you should decide upon your companions for your outing and should select the scene of your camping operations.

Many people are excellent companions in the city, or even on a pleasure trip, a motor tour or a yachting cruise, who are impossible when camping out. Avoid going camping with irritable, impatient, lazy, super-sensitive, nervous, peevish, superstitious, or over-fastidious individuals. Don't expect a man who drinks to excess, or one who is lost without his club, his evening clothes or his daily papers, to make a good campmate. Camping calls for old clothes, lack of luxuries and conveniences, primitive life, and unfailing good temper and cheerfulness under all conditions, as well as plenty of hard work and a willingness to do one's share of anything and everything without being asked. Nervous or superstitious people have no place in the woods. A thunder storm, the cry of a wild animal or a night bird, or even the silence of the dark woods may drive a nervous person to distraction, regardless of how much they enjoy the life during the daytime; while superstitious persons will find omens for good or bad in so many perfectly natural occurrences that they become a nuisance to others and are miserable themselves.

Over-indulgence in liquor is bad enough anywhere, but in the woods, or in camps, it is a real menace. Irritable individuals will find plenty to complain about, even in the best regulated camps, and patience is a prime necessity when one is camping out. One must take things as they are, not as one would wish, when in the woods, and the man or woman who is disgusted if insects or twigs get into one's food, or who cannot enjoy a meal served in tin plates and with the ground for a dining table, or who cannot sleep without sheets and soft pillows, or who cannot put up with the thousand and one inconveniences and petty annoyances of primitive life; will find no pleasure and no enjoyment in camping out and will make life miserable for every one else.

Above all avoid the shirker—the lazy individual—as you would the plague. After a long day's tramp there is camp to be made, firewood to be cut, fires to be built, food to be cooked, and many other chores to be done, and the fellow who throws himself upon the ground and takes his ease, while his comrades do the hard and necessary work, is no sort of a chap to have along. If a camping trip is to be enjoyable and a success, each member of the party must do his or her share of labour, and all must be willing to work for the common good; it is a communistic life and there is no place for a shirker.

Of course in a permanent camp the duties may be simplified and equally divided and each member may have his or her own regular work to do. Even where the days are spent in tramping or travelling and camps are made each night, it is a good plan to have certain duties allotted to certain members of the party. One will be a better axeman than another, one will be a better forager, another a better cook, etc. Even when there are but two in the party it saves much discussion and friction if each knows he has certain definite duties of his own, and moreover the work is made easier and quicker when such an arrangement is made. In every camp there will be trials and disappointments, bad weather and hard work. If these are taken good-naturedly and smilingly and are overcome, they will prove but an added zest to the outing. Make the best of everything and do your share, is the first and invariable rule of life in the woods.

When you have selected your companions the next important matter is to choose a leader, for without a head, without some one to direct, the trip will surely be a failure.

For a leader select the one who has had the most experience in out-of-door life and wood-craft, and if there is no one in the party who has had experience in such matters choose the one who is the most practical, who is the calmest and the best natured, and who possesses sound judgment. In other words, one to whom you would naturally look for leadership in any undertaking.

Having selected the various members of the party and their leader, all should make up their minds to follow his directions and abide by his decisions implicitly, unless he shows himself ignorant, overbearing or incompetent. Nevertheless, it's a good plan always to hold a council or meeting when any question arises and if the majority of the party do not agree with the leader he should waive his authority. But of course this does *not* apply to questions where practical knowledge or experience justifies the leader in overruling the ideas of his companions or where he feels that his companions are endangered by their ignorance of conditions.

OUTFITS

The question of campmates and leader being settled, the most important matter to be considered is that of outfit. By outfit I mean clothing, provisions, camp-kits, tools, weapons and in fact everything which is to be taken on the trip. But here again enters the question of where you are to camp, the character of the country and the length of time you are to be away, and whether you are to tramp, motor, canoe or travel by wagon.

Moreover, tastes differ; some people are willing to "tote" more than others for the sake of greater comfort, and a great deal depends upon the amount of money one is willing to spend. If you are to camp within easy reach of settlements or villages, near a well-travelled road or on the shores of a lake or river, or are to have a permanent camp, almost any amount of luxuries and conveniences may be taken along. On the other hand, if you are to tramp and make camp where fancy wills, you should cut down your outfit to the barest necessities. Even the lightest of loads will feel heavy enough to make your back and shoulders ache at the end of a day's tramp through the woods, and one really needs very little.

An experienced woodsman will get along very comfortably with a knife and axe for tools, a tin pie-plate for cooking and eating utensils, a box of matches, some flour, coffee and bacon and the clothing he wears, but the amateur will scarcely be able to get on with such an outfit.

It is unwise to divide up the outfit for several people and allow a definite amount to each one and it's much better for every member of the party to carry his or her own personal belongings with the exception of certain things which must be for common use. It's not necessary to carry as many axes as there are people, nor as many guns, etc., and the food can be added to the loads of those who are not burdened with axes, firearms and similar articles. If there is one outfit for the crowd and this is divided up among the individual members there will always be complaint or dissatisfaction, for some one is bound to think his load is more than his share. If each one totes his own outfit, however, he has only himself to blame for its weight.

The first and most important item of an outfit is the pack in which the goods are to be carried. There is an endless number of styles of packs on the market and each section of the country has its favourite. Some old campaigners prefer birch bark boxes or baskets, others knapsacks, others blanket rolls similar to those used by soldiers, others swear by baskets and still others think nothing equals the canvas pack of the north woods. So, too, the method of carrying differs. Indians, and many white guides as well, carry heavy loads upon their backs supported by a band across the forehead; others support their loads entirely from their shoulders, while others use shoulder and chest straps. Personally, I prefer the simple canvas pack with shoulder and breast straps and I have tried nearly every type known. This style of pack (*Fig. 1*) may be purchased ready-made for about $3, but they are very simple and may easily be made at home from stout canvas, khaki, or cotton drill. The size depends largely upon the amount you wish to carry and your own size, but 16x24 inches square and 8 inches deep is large enough, and for boys' use a pack 14x20x6 will be ample. Such a pack will easily hold everything one really needs for a long trip and when filled will weigh all you'll want to carry on a day's tramp.

Aside from the pack you will require axes— one if there are but two in the party and two or more if there are a number of campers. Don't try to economise on the axe; it's a mighty important item and the very best axe you can purchase should be selected. Don't make the mistake of getting an axe either too large or too small. Hatchets come in handy, but a good two pound or two-and-a-half pound axe with full length handle is the best and most useful tool you can have in a timbered country. Another extremely useful tool, especially in a brushy country, is the machete—the long heavy-bladed knife of Latin America (*Fig. 2*). Where there are two or more in the party it's a good plan for one to carry an axe, another a machete and another a hatchet, for each tool has its uses and advantages. In many districts a machete is almost a necessity, and if I were compelled to choose between an axe or a machete for all around use, I'd take the machete every time. This instrument, in the hands of one accustomed to its use, will serve almost any purpose from that of an axe to a toothpick. They are ideal for cutting brush, vines and brambles, for blazing trees, for opening a trail and for lopping off branches and even large trees may be felled with a machete when you know how to handle it. They are light and easily carried, are handier than an axe or hatchet and are cheap, costing with sheath about $2.

For the balance of your outfit, aside from clothing and provisions, the following should be included, but of course some items may be omitted and others added according to conditions. In a fishless district it obviously would be useless to

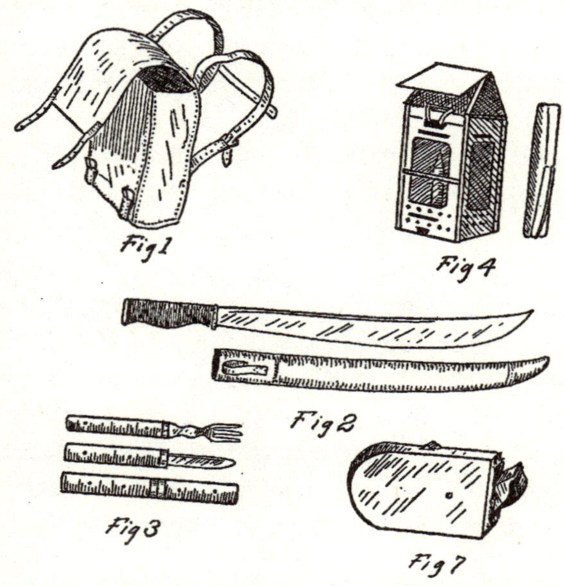

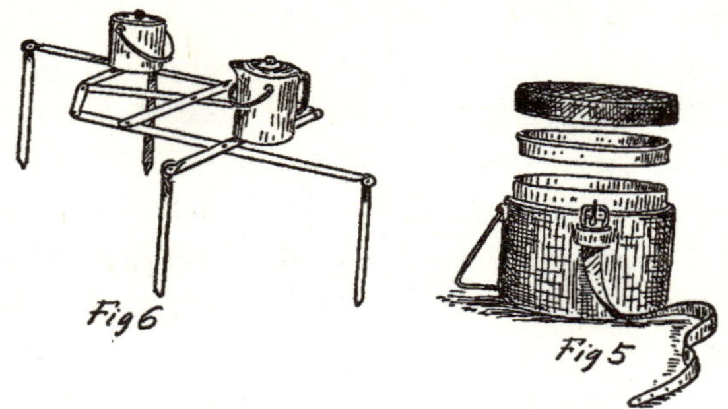

Fig 6

Fig 5

carry fishing tackle; where there is no game, or where laws prevent shooting or trapping, guns and ammunition are unnecessary, and many of the articles will serve for the entire party.

A waterproof cylindrical matchsafe and matches.

A combination knife and fork (*Fig. 3*) or a common steel knife and fork.

A teaspoon and a tablespoon.

A good axe-stone, preferably a carborundum stone.

A bag containing thread, needles, wax, buttons, pins, shoelaces, etc.

A roll, or hank, of good strong line, or braided cotton twine.

Fish hooks, lines and sinkers.

A reliable pocket compass.

A good heavy knife, a sailor's sheath knife is excellent.

A folding rubber, or collapsible, drinking cup.

A tin cup and a deep tin pie-plate.

Half a dozen or more candles.

Some assorted or mixed wire nails from 3 to 12 penny.

All the above are individual necessities and in addition you should of course have a hair-brush and comb, toothbrush, shaving utensils—if you intend to shave—and a small pocket mirror. The latter will prove very useful if you get something in your eye; it is valuable for signalling and is more convenient than a pool of water.

If you are alone, or if there are several in the party, the following should be provided but where there are two or more campers these articles need not be duplicated, but may be for common use:

About one hundred feet of light, strong rope— braided is the best. A medicine case and emergency kit.

The rope will weigh little and should be strong enough to bear the weight of any member of the party with safety. It invariably should be kept neatly coiled and ready for use as it may save human life more than once and will prove invaluable in a hundred places and a thousand ways.

You may tramp, camp and live in the woods for years and never have occasion to use medicines, stimulants, bandages or first-aid, but accidents *will* happen and when you *are* hurt or sick in the woods a bit of medicine, a bandage or some other simple remedy or aid will be worth more than all the rest of your outfit put together.

Old campers and woodsmen may pooh-pooh the idea of a medicine kit, but many a life would have been saved if such men always carried simple remedies and first-aid outfits. On more than one occasion I have saved my own life by means of a pocket emergency case and more than one old woodsman has thanked God I carried it with me. If there are several in the party, have one member in charge of the medicines day and night, and allow no one else to handle it, save in case of emergency. In this way you'll always know where the things are when you want them and when you *do* want them you'll want them in a hurry.

The exact contents of such a kit depends upon the country and the trip, for certain districts have certain diseases and certain insects, and accidents are more liable to occur in some places and under some conditions than in others. Avoid liquid medicines as far as possible and use tablets and pills. The following is a list of the most important things for the kit and will be found very satisfactory for all around use in most places and under ordinary conditions.

Quinine pills or tablets
Rhubarb pills or tablets
Bicarbonate of soda or soda-mint tablets
Bismuth subnitrate
Chlorate of potash
Warburg's tincture
Sun cholera pills
Several rolls of antiseptic bandages
A box of zinc ointment
A bottle of Zeroform or Iodoform
Permanganate of potash
Some powerful stimulant

Adhesive surgeons' plaster (Red Cross is good) but *not* courtplaster.

The most convenient form in which to carry these is in the little pocket leather cases that cost from $1 to $5 each.

If you object to alcoholic stimulants take your physician's advice as to what to carry to take its place, and if you don't believe in medicine yourself carry the outfit for the benefit of those who do. Moreover, your ideas may change suddenly if you are taken ill or are injured far from civilisation.

A stimulant may save a life if one of the party is nearly drowned or faint from loss of blood or a broken limb. The permanganate of potash dissolved in water will relieve pain from insect bites and ivy poison, and where poisonous snakes occur it is the best and safest remedy known for their bites. Antiseptic tablets are good things to have along, for a very slight scratch, cut, or bruise may result seriously if neglected, and an ounce of prevention is worth countless tons of cure in the woods. Be sure and have everything labelled and mark all poisons in *heavy black letters and with a skull and bones.* If you are not accustomed to using medicines have your physician give you directions for using the various remedies and keep written directions in the case with the medicines.

In addition to all the above there are many other light, simple and cheap articles which will add greatly to the enjoyment of camp life and

which you may take or not as you choose. Such
are folding lanterns (*Fig. 4*) of mica and aluminum and costing about $1.50 each and which
weigh but a few ounces and fold flat in compact
form when not in use. Japanese messkits (*Fig.
5*) which cost about $2 and are very convenient
as they are made of aluminum and fold into very
small space. Campfire grates (*Fig. 6*) which
cost $1 and save many spilled cups of coffee and
many a burned pancake. These are but a few
of the numerous handy articles which any dealer
in sporting goods and campers' outfits can supply. But don't load yourself down and clutter
yourself up with a lot of these things—there is
no end to them—unless you are going by canoe,
auto or other conveyance, or are planning to stay
in one spot for some time.

I have mentioned a match box, but under the
best of conditions and with every precaution,
matches will at times get wet and useless, and
hence it is a wise plan to provide against such a
contingency. In another chapter I will explain
how to build fires without matches, but a very
simple and useful article which will save much
trouble and annoyance is a mechanical lighter
(*Fig. 7*). Do not carry one of the lighters
which must be filled with gasoline or alcohol but
the kind which uses a plain cotton fuse or tinder.
With such a tinder a fire may be kindled with a
flint and steel, but the tinder should invariably
be carried in a water-tight metal box. For match
boxes use rubber rather than metal for these will

float if dropped overboard.

The pie plate and tin cup will do very well for all cooking purposes; the plate serving as a frying plan or skillet by providing it with a handle made by splitting the end of a stick, slipping it over the edge of the plate and driving a nail through it, while the cup will serve to cook coffee, boil eggs or even make a stew.

But of course, if you wish, you can carry other cooking utensils *ad libitum*, especially if you don't depend upon shank's mare for your transportation.

CLOTHING

To many, especially those who are new at camping, the matter of clothing is of very great moment. The average prospective camper looks over the catalogue of some sporting goods' dealer and finds that the beautifully made and exceedingly expensive clothing will cost more than all the rest of the outfit, or even more than the whole trip. This is a great mistake. The woods are no place for fancy dress, and as a rule the high-priced clothing designed—ostensibly—for camping, is impractical and utterly worthless for real, dyed-in-the-wool roughing it. Provide the stoutest, most comfortable and cheapest things possible. Khaki is good, but any stout, easy garments will serve every purpose. Don't mind if they are old, stained or worn—by the time you've been in the woods a week you'll never know the difference. Use woollen undergarments—in the woods one is often wet and dry by turns and cotton is worthless under such conditions. Stout easy shoes or knee-boots should be worn and moccasins will be found very comfortable about camp, when canoeing or in a dry country. If you are going to a rocky, mountainous district or must ford streams, have hob-nails in your boots and see that your footgear is *always* kept well greased and soft and pliable. Carry at least one change of undergarments, one of outer clothing if you can manage it, and plenty of socks or stockings. Blankets are not essential, although comfortable and useful. A light, all-wool blanket and a very light rubber blanket add greatly to one's health and comfort and don't add much to the load, and if you are travelling by canoe or other conveyance by all means take blankets along. If the rubber blanket has a slit in the centre—with the edges bound with tape to prevent tearing—it will serve for a cape or poncho by slipping it over your head. Mosquito head nets should also be included if you are to camp where gnats, sand flies, black flies or mosquitos are found, and there are mighty few places in the woods where these pests don't swarm in summer.

No two people can agree as to the amount of clothes they need and each must suit himself in this matter; the main thing is to be warm, comfortable and well protected, and of all things be sure that your footgear does not cramp, blister or chafe your feet. Don't start off with new shoes and don't wear silk socks or thin socks. Good, heavy wool is the best material. What you want is durability and comfort, not appearance.

Finally comes the matter of provisions. If you are going into a good fish or game country you will not require such a large stock or variety of food as in a district where you cannot hunt or fish to eke out your larder. If there are farm houses or villages within reach you can get along with even less, whereas, if you are travelling up rivers or over watercourses by canoe or boat, or are going to your camping place by vehicle, take along all you can conveniently carry. No hard or fast rule can be given as to the provisions you'll require or the articles which are most essential, aside from coffee, sugar, salt, lard (or cottolene), pepper, bacon, salt pork and a few such things which are about as necessary to camp life as an axe or matches.

But the following are all excellent, reliable, useful things and will serve as a guide to what camp provisions should consist of:

Erbswurst. A composition of pea-meal, meat and vegetables compressed into a sausage-shaped roll and adopted by nearly all armies as the nearest approach to a perfect, all-around food. May be eaten raw or cooked in many ways.

Soup Tablets. Various styles and flavours and very useful. Dissolved in hot water they form a delicious soup which can be prepared in a few moments.

Dried Vegetables. Best of vegetables evaporated and compressed. Equal to ten or twelve times their weight in fresh vegetables and are easily prepared. Potatoes, beans, spinach, carrots, cabbage, celery, onions, leeks, turnips, parsnips and many other varieties. By far the best form in which to carry vegetables.

Truemilk. A dried milk and superior to evaporated or condensed milk for camping purposes.

Army Bread or "Hardtack" is the best form of breadstuff for a camp trip.

Truegg, or dried eggs, are delicious and most convenient. Made from strictly fresh eggs beaten, evaporated and with all the properties of fresh eggs. Dissolved in water before using. Can be made into omelettes, scrambled eggs, etc., and will keep in any climate. One pound equals four dozen fresh eggs.

Crystalose, is more compact and convenient than sugar, but does not possess all the properties of sugar. Useful where the outfit must be limited and everything reduced to the least possible weight.

I have often been asked how much food should be carried per person on a camping trip. This is one of the most difficult questions to answer, for appetites vary and what would be ample for one person might leave another half starved. The following has been decided upon by many experienced woodsmen as the quantity of food required for one individual for two weeks. If you are a light eater you can take less, if a heavy eater, more; but don't forget that your appetite will increase in the woods and *don't* overlook the possibilities of fish, game and farmers' supplies. If you err either way, take too much rather than too little however; in fact my advice is to take *all* you can carry. Even if it does weigh a lot at the beginning you can console yourself with the thought that it will grow lighter each day.

Flour or its equivalents,	6 lbs.
Corn Meal,	2 lbs.
Beans,	2 lbs.
Erbswurst,	¼ lb.
Soup Tablets,	½ lb.
Sugar,	2 lbs.
Baking Powder,	¼ lb.
Coffee,	½ lb.
Butter,	1 lb.
Saltpork,	2½ lbs.
Evaporated Milk,	1½ lbs.
Dried Fruits,	1 lb.
Salt,	¼ lb.
Chocolate or cocoa	¼ lb.
Tea,	¼ lb.
Bacon,	1½ lbs.
Dried Potatoes,	1 lb.
Dried Vegetables,	½ lb.
Dried Eggs,	1¼ lbs.
Shelled Nuts,	½ lb.

By all means provide a supply of sweet or milk chocolate. It is one of the best and most nourishing of foods. A small cake of chocolate will keep one from hunger and fatigue in a marvellous manner and I have often tramped from dawn until dark with no other food than a cake of sweet chocolate. Nuts are also very compact food and peanut butter is excellent. Carry all flour and dry groceries in waterproof bags, for tins are cumbersome and are hard to pack well. Bags for this purpose may be made easily from waterproof canvas which can be purchased of any dealer in tents or sporting goods.

At last, when you have selected your clothing, have obtained your outfit and have decided upon your provisions, weigh them and find how much of a load you've to carry. The probability is that it will be a great deal more than you expected, but don't be discouraged unless you *know* you are not strong enough to carry it. Of course if it won't all go in the pack, or if it weighs a great deal, you will have to eliminate certain things, that is, if you are going to tramp with all your earthly camping possessions on your back; but if you are going by canoe or vehicle, the weight won't matter much. But even when "hoofing it," it will surprise you to find how much you can carry. When I was a boy of sixteen I spent a summer camping and trapping through the mountains of northern New Hampshire, and my regular load was fifty pounds. Some of the natives—fishermen and trappers—carried as much as one hundred pounds, but as a rule thirty-five pounds is all you'll want to tote until you become accustomed to it and one can get a surprising amount of dunnage into a thirty-five pound pack.

CHAPTER II

HOW AND WHERE TO CAMP

VERY often camp life is made miserable and an outing is a failure merely because the spot selected for a campsite is unsuitable. Many people seem to think that one can make camp at any old place, but this is a grave mistake. To be sure, temporary, one-night camps need not be selected with the same care as permanent camps, but there are certain things essential to camping which should *always* be sought. An old woodsman apparently makes camp wherever the humour suits him or nightfall finds him, but in reality he uses keen judgment and foresight and selects the spot for his camp with reference to its location and surroundings. But the experienced woodsman sees and realises these things instinctively, or else knows through long experience where to look for them, and intuitively seeks the right spot. To the amateur it's quite a different matter, and one place may appear quite as good as another; and, moreover, he seldom can judge "by the lay of the land" where to look for the essential requirements of a good campsite. As a result it often requires some time and not often a little search to find a suitable spot in which to camp, and hence you should not wait until too late in the day to make camp, but should leave yourself plenty of time to find a place fulfilling all, or as many as possible, of your requirements.

Of course in a dry, barren country where there is no water, or in an open treeless country, the following rules do not apply, but one seldom selects such situations for camping and as a rule camps for pleasure are made in well-timbered, well-watered districts. The two prime essentials for a campsite are wood and water. Not necessarily a large body of water nor heavy forest, but good drinking water, such as a brook or spring, and with enough timber to furnish shelter and fire. Given these, you should select fairly high, well-drained land, preferably a knoll or hillock, for a hollow or depression is always damp and chilly and a heavy rain during the night may flood the camp. Avoid rocky or stony ground—granite makes uncomfortable beds and it's next to impossible to drive sticks or erect a strong camp on ledges or where rocks are covered by a thin layer of soil. Don't camp in a pine or hemlock grove if you can help it. Fire will creep and spread in the fallen pine needles or hemlock leaves and a forest fire may result, but *do* select a spot where hemlocks, spruce, firs or other evergreens are near at hand for these trees are of the greatest value to the camper. You *may* have to camp on a hillside, but if you do, don't fail to dig a trench around the upper side of your camp to carry off the water in case it rains and thus avoid being flooded out.

Don't pitch your tent or build your camp too close to the edge of a pond, lake or stream; they may rise during the night and you'll wake up to find yourself in several inches of ice-cold water. Don't select a spot overgrown with thick brush or weeds. It's a tiresome job to clear this away and your time can be spent to better advantage. If possible, select a location where there is fallen timber or dead trees near at hand as this will save much weary work chopping and burning green wood. If there are white birches in the vicinity so much the better; birch bark is a very useful article to the camper. If you are travelling by canoe choose a spot as handy to your landing place as possible. If you are touring and camping by automobile try to locate a camp site within reach of the road and your car. If you are using a tent you can pitch it anywhere, as long as there is good drainage, drinking water, firm ground for your tent pegs and wood for fuel. If you don't wish to be troubled by mosquitos and other insect pests select a spot which is open to the sun during the day and where the breeze has a clear sweep at night, but *don't* pitch your camp to leeward of the fire, unless you wish to be kept awake all night by smoke with the chance of having the camp burned down if the wind rises.

THE BEST CAMP TO USE

As I have already mentioned, there is no *best* camp for all purposes or for all places. The particular kind of camp to be used depends very largely upon conditions, and what might be the best camp in one place or for one purpose might be the very worst type under other conditions or in another locality. There is every gradation of camp, from a mere shelter of boughs or branches to the elaborate comfortable log cabin, and there are styles and forms of tents without number.

It is scarcely necessary to describe tents. Each camper who decides to use a tent must determine upon its size and pattern for himself, but personally I consider the "A" and "wall-tents" the best forms. Where there are but one or two persons the "A" tent will serve every purpose, but if there are several in the party or a more substantial camp for a long stay is desired, the "wall-tent" is preferable. Before pitching a tent, clear up the ground where you intend to place it and for some distance around on all sides. With an axe, hatchet or machete this is easily done. Bend over the bushes and young saplings with one hand and chop through the strained fibres close to the ground and you will find that even good sized trees may readily be cut off with a few sharp blows. After the tent is pitched, the ground within should be smoothed and softened. Pull up all twigs, roots and small stubs, remove the dead leaves and trash and with the back of the axe—used like an adze by swinging it between your legs—knock down all the knobs and hummocks of earth until the surface is smooth and level. Perhaps you think this an unnecessary labour, but if you sleep all night on two or three lumps of earth or a small pebble or a sharp stick you'll wish you'd spent an hour or so smoothing the ground.

If you are using a "wall"- or "A" tent, try to

find a spot where there are two trees, ten or more feet apart, and stretch a rope between them for the ridge pole of your tent or, if preferred, place a strong sapling between the trees instead of using the rope. If there are projecting branches or crotches on the trees the pole may be laid in these, but if not—and it's seldom that two trees have branches exactly the same height above the ground —the pole may be lashed in place by rope or withes. The rope ridge is, however, the most convenient for it's always on hand and when not in use may be wrapped around the tent. Don't mind if the rope sags when the tent is thrown over it, that will be remedied later. Next make your tent-pegs—unless you carry steel pegs with you, which is a good plan if you have a canoe or motor car, but adds unnecessary weight if you are tramping. To make tent-pegs easily and quickly, place a young maple or birch sapling—about an inch in diameter—across a log and by two sharp blows, at an angle, cut off sections at least 18 inches long. These long pegs will prevent the ropes from slipping off and will hold the ground far better than shorter ones. Throw the tent over the ridge, peg down the four corners, and be sure to get them square and equidistant from the ridge and one another. Peg down the edges of the tent and then cut a crotched stick, a trifle longer than the height of your tent in the centre. Wedge this under the ridge rope in the centre of the tent and it will draw all sides of the tent tight and smooth. If a few projecting branch stubs are left on this upright stick they'll serve a useful purpose to hang things on. If the ground is rocky or thin you may have trouble in driving pegs. In that case drive them at a sharp angle and pile flat rocks on top of them, or place good sized logs against them on the side nearest the tent. They will hold even in a gale when thus secured.

But it's far more fun to build your own camp than to put up a tent and it takes but little more time, while a well-built camp is just as secure and comfortable as a tent.

Probably the best in most places is the kind shown as a "lean-to." To build a lean-to is one of the very first and most important things you should learn, for no one can consider himself a woodsman or a camper until he can erect a weatherproof, substantial lean-to from the materials at his command in the forest.

Although the lean-to is primarily adapted to one night or temporary camps, yet it is an easy matter to build a lean-to strong and substantial enough to be used as a permanent camp for a whole summer; the principle being identical in either case. It's such an easy matter to build a lean-to that almost any one who can use an axe or hatchet should have no difficulty, but just the same it will save a lot of time and trouble if you practise the art in woods near home before starting off on your camping trip. This will not only save time, but you'll become accustomed to using your simple tools and you'll learn which materials are best adapted to your purposes and where to find them, and you'll acquire many a little "wrinkle" and get the "knack" of building your camp without unnecessary labour and wasted energy.

After you have found a suitable camping spot select a pair of strong trees eight to twelve feet apart—the size of your camp will of course depend upon the number of campers—and with branches six to eight feet above the ground. If you can't find two such trees you need not be discouraged for poles may be lashed to the trunks instead of resting them on limbs and, by using a stouter cross-piece, trees twenty feet apart may be used.

But assuming that you have found two such trees, proceed to clear the ground between them and for the space you intend for the floor of your camp, as directed for pitching a tent. Next cut three or four poles about twelve feet long and at least three inches in diameter at the larger ends. Place one of these across the two standing trees—resting the ends in crotches of the branches where they join the trunks, or lashing them to the trunks, at a height of five to eight feet above the ground according to the size of the lean-to that you wish to build. (*Fig. 1.*) Then place two other poles with their large ends resting on the ground and their small ends resting on the pole between the trees as shown in *Fig. 2.* Be sure these two poles are parallel and extend the same distance from the cross-piece between the trees. And here it may be well to state that the cross-piece between the trees will be the front of the camp and that the fire is to be built before it and hence the spot should be chosen and the camp built with reference to this.

Between the two slanting poles place a number of smaller poles parallel with them. (*Fig. 3.*) Don't make the mistake of trimming off the branches from these poles so they are smooth. Leave little stubs about two or three inches long as these are very useful, or even necessary. Across these slanting poles, and resting against the projecting stubs, lay a number of light poles or branches (*Fig. 4*) and the frame of the lean-to is complete. To form the roof you may either thatch it or use bark. If there are plenty of evergreens about, thatching is the best and easiest method, especially for a temporary camp, but bark —especially birch bark—makes a tighter roof and is advisable for a permanent camp. If there are two campers one should be gathering thatch material while the other erects the framework; if there are three in the party the third may be gathering firewood and preparing the evening meal, and if there are more than three all can take hold and by doing various things at the same time camp will be built as if by magic.

For the thatch select large flat "fans" or tips, of soft, thick hemlock or fir boughs. Commencing at the lower end of the slanting room hook these fans over the cross-pieces in layers like shingles, with each layer overlapping the ones below it. (*Fig. 5.*) Continue in this way until the roof is completely covered, and if you wish still better protection place a second or third layer over the first.   If it's windy or stormy place additional poles over the thatch—running them parallel with the slanting roof-poles and lash them in place with hemlock roots, withes or twine.   If you wish still greater security and shelter place upright poles extending from the ground to the roof poles, place horizontal poles across these and thatch them as you did the roof.   Very often two lean-tos are built near together and facing each other and

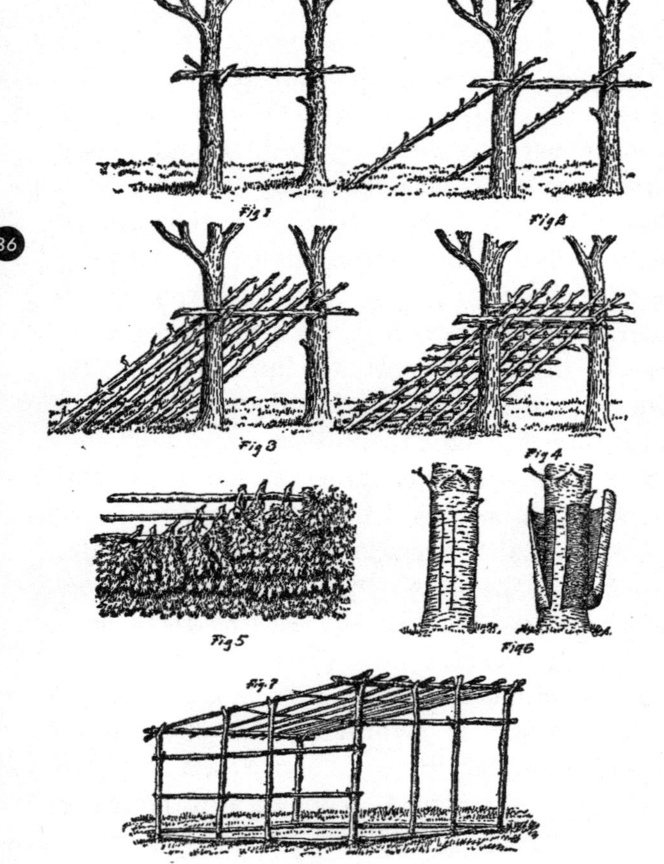

the fire is then built between them. This arrangement makes a very comfortable camp and one half may be used during the day and the other for sleeping or both may be used for sleeping quarters if there are several persons in the party. A very comfortable permanent camp may be built in this way and enclosing one side of the opening between the two lean-tos, and if desired it may also be roofed, in which case the fire must be built outside.

In case you cannot find evergreen trees handy, or if you wish an even more substantial roof, peel bark from birch trees or hemlocks and use the sheets like shingles—securing them in position by means of poles laid across them and lashed in place. But don't sacrifice trees and leave them to die for the sake of their bark. It isn't necessary and by peeling the bark properly the trees will continue to live and grow and will soon recover from their injuries. The idea is to leave a narrow, continuous strip of bark, so that the sap may find its way up the tree, which it cannot do if the bark is peeled from the entire circumference of the trees.

To peel the bark properly make two cuts nearly, but not quite, around the tree—one as high as you can reach, the other near the ground. Connect the ends of these cuts by perpendicular incisions (*Fig. 6*) and by starting the bark at one of these the whole slab will come off, leaving the narrow strip on one side of the tree untouched. If there are branches, stubs or twigs on the part selected they should be cut close and flush with the trunk before starting to peel the bark as otherwise the piece of bark will be torn and ripped as you peel it off.

After the lean-to is built, smooth the ground within it as already directed, and then you may busy yourself making the beds.

Although a lean-to may be thrown together in less than an hour, yet such hastily constructed camps are intended only for temporary shelters, or for a single night's use. But a lean-to may be built with care which will be practically waterproof and will withstand the heaviest storms and wettest weather and will last for several seasons. If made with a heavy, strongly built framework securely lashed together, and covered with birch or hemlock bark held in place by light poles lashed across the sheets, a lean-to may be made tight and snug enough for midwinter use.

Another method of making a very warm and comfortable camp is to build two lean-tos a short distance apart and with their open sides facing each other. Then, by building the fire between the two, the heat will be thrown into both shelters and there will be no chance for cold air to enter.

But in many places there are no suitable trees for the purpose of making a lean-to, or else, one can not cut timber at will, and in such localities, the camper may resort to some other form of shack. Shacks or huts may be made of almost any material, such as grass, reeds, branches, brush, straw or hay.   They may be mere shelters for one night and roughly built or they may be substantial snug houses of "wattled" or "thatched" construction.   A well-made wattled or thatched shack is wind, water and storm proof, cool in summer and warm in winter and in many parts of the world the natives use such huts for permanent residences.   They are especially valuable in warm climates, and where there is abundant material for their construction, they can be readily and rapidly built.

Wattled shacks may be built of small boughs or withes of almost any sort, such as willow, hazel, birch, etc., for a frame and may be covered with any handy material, such as straw, grass, hay, cattails, reeds, tules, bullrushes or evergreen boughs or a combination of several.

The first step is to erect a rough framework of the desired size (*Fig. 7*).   This may be of branches, poles, fence rails or sticks of any kind and the various pieces may be lashed together with withes, roots, vines, twisted straw or grass, twine or thongs, or nails may be used, as preferred.   As the wattling will strengthen and stiffen the whole, the frame may be very light and flimsy, although if the hut is to serve as a permanent camp or for some time, it is wise to make the frame carefully and strongly of good sized, rigid material.   When the frame is completed the next thing is to attach poles or sticks reaching from the upper edge of the frame to the ground as illustrated in *Fig. 8*.   These vertical poles should be spaced three or four inches apart and openings should be left for such doors and windows as you may desire, as shown in the cut. Then, with flexible branches, roots, withes, wisps of grass or straw, reeds, or whatever material is the handiest, weave under and over the vertical poles in a sort of rough basket work as shown in *Fig. 9.* It may seem as if this would be a slow and tedious job, but you will find that with plenty of material on hand, the work will proceed very rapidly and you will be surprised to find how soon a good sized frame may be covered.

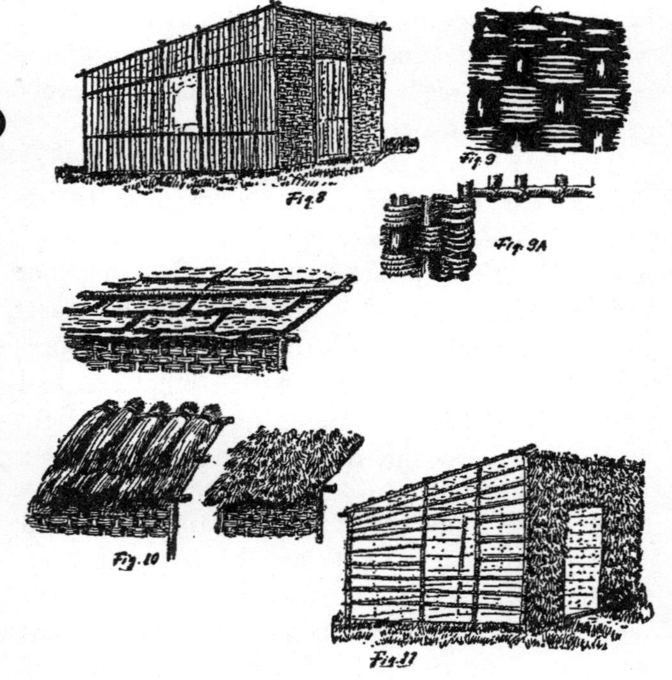

Where the wattling reaches the edges of door and window openings, the material should be bent around the poles and tucked back under and over one or two poles as in *Fig. 9 A.*

When the walls are covered, wattle the roof in the same manner and finish it by laying slabs of bark, bunches of grass or rushes, or evergreen permanent camp or for some time, it is wise to make the frame carefully and strongly of good sized, rigid material. When the frame is completed the next thing is to attach poles or sticks reaching from the upper edge of the frame to the ground as illustrated in *Fig. 8.* These vertical poles should be spaced three or four inches apart and openings should be left for such doors and windows as you may desire, as shown in the cut. Then, with flexible branches, roots, withes, wisps of grass or straw, reeds, or whatever material is the handiest, weave under and over the vertical poles in a sort of rough basket work as shown in *Fig. 9.* It may seem as if this would be a slow and tedious job, but you will find that with plenty of material on hand, the work will proceed very rapidly and you will be surprised to find how soon a good sized frame may be covered.

Fig 11 B.

Where the wattling reaches the edges of door and window openings, the material should be bent around the poles and tucked back under and over one or two poles as in *Fig. 9 A*.

When the walls are covered, wattle the roof in the same manner and finish it by laying slabs of bark, bunches of grass or rushes, or evergreen boughs over it. Place the lowest layer first and let each succeeding layer overlap those below like shingles (*Fig. 10*). If a sufficient "pitch" or slant has been given to the roof frame this covering will be perfectly waterproof, even in the heaviest rains.

No doubt your first attempts at wattling will be rather crude and there will be numerous openings between the poles and wattling material, but these may be rendered water and wind tight by daubing the whole surface with mud or clay, or the crevices may be chinked with moss, sod, grass or other material.

Doors may be constructed of canvas or may be made of a frame covered with wattling and the windows may be closed with shutters made in the same manner. If there are any tough, flexible withes, roots or vines available, the doors and shutters may be hung with such material to serve as hinges. Even twisted wisps of grass or straw or braided reeds will answer this purpose. Another method of building shacks is by "thatching," which is a very easy method when grass, reeds, straw or rushes are abundant and withes and bushes are scarce. Even evergreen boughs may be used for thatching, as described in the construction of a lean-to (*Fig. 5*), but straw, grass or reeds are the best materials. For a thatched hut construct the framework as described for a wattled hut, but with the light poles lashed *horizontally* instead of *vertically* (*Fig. 11*). Then, commencing at the bottom, lash bunches of the thatching material to these poles, finishing one complete row before placing the next, and being careful that each succeeding row of thatch overlaps the one below and that each bundle of thatch "breaks the joints" of those underneath, as shown in *Fig. 11 B*.

The roof is thatched in the same way and it should be borne in mind that the more closely the bunches of thatch are tied and the more rows there are the tighter will be the roof. Doors and windows may be made of thatched frames or of wattling and a wattled hut may often be provided with a thatched roof to advantage.

Of all permanent camps, the log house is the most substantial, but to build a log cabin one must be an expert axeman and many large trees must be sacrificed and as our forests are being far too rapidly destroyed as it is the large trees should never be cut for the purpose of building a camp unless absolutely necessary.

Sometimes, where lumbering has been carried on, a very good substitute for a log cabin may be constructed from the bark-covered slabs cut from the logs and cast aside as waste by the lumbermen. In some parts of the country sod-houses are in use and where there is an abundant tough sod and one desires a permanent camp a sod house may be built to advantage. The process is so simple as scarcely to require description, for it is as easy as building a snow house. The sods are cut into squares and merely piled one on another to form the walls and the whole is roofed with poles which are also covered with sods, or if preferred, the roof may be thatched.

Still another type of camp which has some advantages is the Indian tepee, and while tepees may perhaps be classed as tents rather than as shacks, yet a tepee may be built of poles and covered with sheets of bark, wattling or thatching. The greatest advantage of the tepee is the ease with which it may be set up, taken down and carried from place to place. Moreover it is far better ventilated, more comfortable and more thoroughly weatherproof than most forms of tents. Its disadvantages are that long poles must be carried if the tepee is to be used in a district where poles cannot be cut as desired while its circular floor plan does not accommodate itself to economy of space as readily as the square or rectangular shape of other tents. But in the minds of many its advantages more than outweigh its disadvantages and for all around use there are few tents more convenient and portable than the tepee. It is a difficult matter to purchase ready made tepees which are really good and many are mere playthings, suitable only for lawns or gardens, and it is far more satisfactory to make one's own tepees, which is a very simple matter.

The size of the tepee to be used will depend upon the number of persons who are to occupy it as well as upon the distance it is to be carried and the means of transportation. A tepee 14 feet in height and with a floor 14 feet in diameter is large enough for three or four occupants and is about as large as can readily be carried afoot or in a small canoe.

To make a tepee of these dimensions will require fifty yards of cloth and the material used will depend upon your own taste and pocket book. Cotton drill, light canvas, waterproof silk, khaki or any other tent fabric may be used. The breadths of cloth should first be sewed together to form a rectangular sheet 10 yards long by 5 yards in width and with each edge lapped and double stitched as shown in *Fig. 12 A*. Stretch this piece of cloth upon a smooth, level surface, mark the exact centre of one of the long edges and drive a nail at the spot (*Fig. 12*x) secure a piece of strong twine or cord and tie a small loop in each end, so that from centre to centre of the loops is 15 feet. Place one loop over the nail and in the other loop insert a piece of charcoal, a soft pencil or a coloured crayon, and while holding the cord tight, draw a half circle on the cloth as at C-D *Fig. 12*. At the places marked E-E cut out triangular spaces each 10 inches deep and 10 inches wide and mark off a space of 7 feet 8 inches from D-G and from C-F and divide each of these spaces into eight equal parts of

11½ inches.   On each of these marks make two small circles or dots 2 inches apart and with the outer ones 2 inches from the edge of the cloth.   Then mark off 25 spaces 2 feet apart along the curved line from C-D.   Then, from the corners of the cloth outside of the semi-circular line, cut a couple of pieces of the form

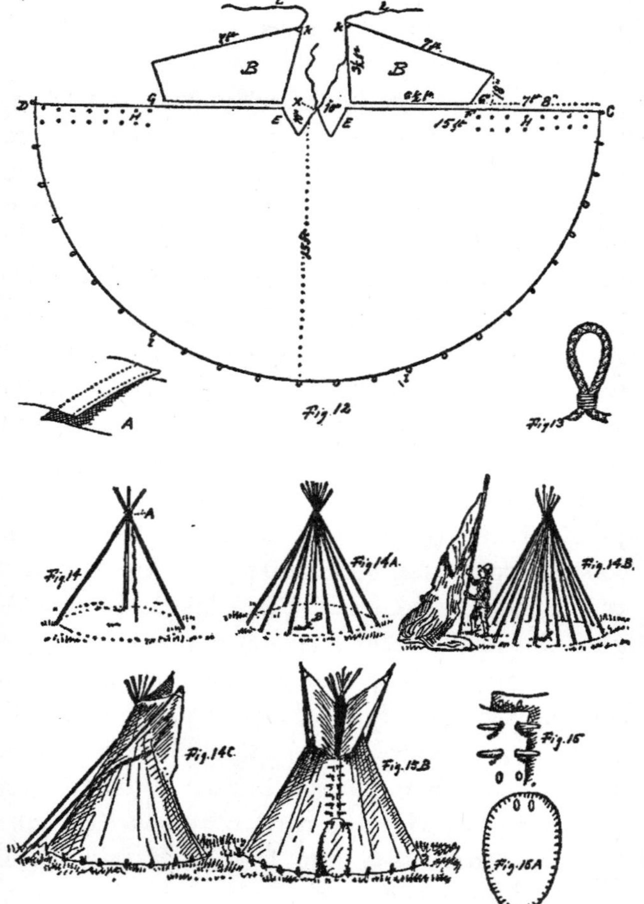

shown in *Fig. 12 B,* each of which should be 7 feet on the long edge, 6½ feet on the short edge, 3½ feet across one end and 1½ feet across the other end. Sew small triangular pieces in one corner of each to form little pockets (K) and attach pieces of strong light rope (L). The cloth may now be cut out around the curved line from C-D and the edges from D-G and from F-C should be hemmed. Around the curve from C-D hem in a light rope, having loops projecting at each of the marks (I). Each of these loops should be about 1½ inches in diameter and should be made by splicing or seizing the rope as illustrated at *Fig. 13.* The edges of the two pieces B B should be neatly hemmed and at each of the marks H, holes should be made through the cloth and the rough edges finished by "buttonhole" stitching. Finally, attach a couple of pieces of rope at the point X, sew the pieces B B in position as shown, and the tepee is ready for use.

In order to set up the tepee twelve straight poles are required, ten of which should be about 16 to 18 feet in length, while the other two should be at least 20 feet long. You will also need about 25 feet of light rope, eight pins of hard wood about 8 inches long and ¼ inch in diameter and 25 tent pegs 1 foot long and 1 inch in diameter. To erect the tepee, tie three of the 16 foot poles together at one end, using a few turns of the 25 foot rope for the purpose, mark a 14 foot circle on the ground and place the poles in the form of a tripod with their bases resting on the circle (*Fig. 14*). Then arrange six more of the poles about the circle, with their upper ends resting against the first three poles, and fasten all securely by winding a couple of turns of the rope about them (*Fig. 14 A*). Drive a stout stake in the centre of the circle, draw the hanging end of the rope tight and fasten it to the stake thus anchoring the pole frame as shown at *b* (*Fig. 14 A*).

Now fasten the rope attached to the cloth at X (*Fig. 12*), to the end of the last 16 foot pole and lift the cloth into place as shown at *Fig. 14 B*. Letting the pole rest against the frame, pull the cloth around the poles and peg the bottom into place by pegs driven through the loops at an angle. The two front edges of the cloth should then be lapped and pinned together by means of the lacing pins through the holes I I as in *Fig. 15.*

Insert the ends of the 20 foot poles in the pockets in the corners of flaps B B and swing the flaps into position, quartering the wind, as indicated at *Fig. 14 C.*

When no fire is burning in the tepee, or in a heavy wind or rain, the flaps should be folded over and held in position by the ropes L L, *Fig. 12,* thus completely closing the opening.

The door of the tepee may be closed by lacing or pinning the edges together, but a better plan is to make a cloth door on a light frame of withes as shown at *Fig. 15 A* and which may be hung to a lacing pin as in *Fig. 15 B*. If a piece of canvas the desired shape and size is made and is provided with eyelets or holes around the edges it may be stretched upon a frame as required and thus the nuisance of carrying the awkward door may be avoided.

As a rule a tepee should be set up facing the east, as the prevailing winds are usually westerly and thus the fire will draw better and, moreover, the door and interior will receive the early morning light and more sunshine. When the smoke flaps are closed in bad weather, or when the wind is easterly and there is trouble in making the fire draw well, the lower edge of the tepee may be lifted slightly and a good draught will be secured. In a country where pegs and lacing pins may be cut from standing timber and poles may be secured as required it is only necessary to carry the rope and cloth, which may be rolled into a compact bundle and tied with the 25 foot anchor rope. Properly made and set up, with a bright fire burning within, a tepee is cosy and warm enough for midwinter use, while in summer it may be kept cool and a free circulation of air insured by lifting the lower edge of the cloth for a foot or so above the ground, leaving it pegged down in three or four spots.

In districts where campers travel by canoe or boat on rivers or lakes very comfortable tents and outfits may be carried and many tents are now made which are specially designed for canoe use.

Another delightful method of travelling about

and camping out is by automobile. A regular
tent and outfit may be carried by motor car or,
if preferred, a camp trailer may be hitched behind the car and in which the complete camp
with cots, cooking utensils, mosquito nets and
all other luxuries are compactly stowed. But
while one may camp very comfortably by such
up-to-date outfits, yet much of the real enjoyment
of "roughing it" is lost and, moreover, the most
attractive and best places to camp are usually
out of reach of motor cars or boats. Most important of all, however, is the fact that when
camping by such means one learns little of woodcraft or of self-reliance and dependence on
nature and in this, after all, lies the greatest
value of camping out.

CHAPTER III

CAMP HOUSEKEEPING

THE first thing to be done after camp is pitched, whether you use a tent, a tepee, a hut, a shack, or a lean-to, is to make the beds. For temporary use this is a very simple and easy matter, and you will be surprised to find what a springy, soft and comfortable bed may be made with no tools save an axe, machete or stout knife, and no materials except a quantity of fir or hemlock boughs.

But it is hopeless to try to make a comfortable bed unless the floor of your camp is smooth, level, soft and free from all stubs, stones and hummocks. For this reason you should take care to follow the directions for smoothing the floor (see Chapter II).

This accomplished, cut down a young hemlock, balsam fir, or other evergreen,—the balsam is the best,—or lop a number of good sized branches from trees, and *pull* off the soft "fans" or flattened tips to the branches. I say "pull," for those which are too large or tough to be pulled off by hand are too large and coarse for bed making.

You may have to walk about quite a little in order to secure an ample supply of fans, but there is no difficulty in carrying them if they are placed criss-cross on the handle of your axe or are hung on a light pole.

Having gathered your supply of material, place a thick layer of the fans on the floor of your camp where the bed is to be, and be careful to place the butt ends towards the foot of the bed (which should be towards the fire) and place the branches with their convex sides uppermost. Now, commencing at the foot of the bed, thrust the butt ends of more fans down through the first layer at a slight angle and letting each succeeding row overlap the ones already placed and this working towards the head of the bed or "thatching," just as if you were covering the roof. In this way you will secure a smooth surface of soft fragrant fans with the tips all turned towards the foot of the bed (*Fig. 1*) and by adding one or more additional layers you can make the bed as thick and soft as you may desire and over this the blankets may be spread as over a mattress. Even if you have no blankets or coverings of any sort you will find this rough and ready bed as delightfully restful as any you ever slept in. The next step is to build a fire, but of course, if there are several people in the camp, work should be arranged so that while some are making the camp others are building the fire and cooking and others are gathering material for the beds, for one of the first rules to be observed when camping is to have each member of the party assigned to a definite duty. Then there will be no bother nor vexatious delays and everything will go along orderly and smoothly with no loss of time or temper. It may seem like a very simple matter to build a fire, and you may think that a description of how to do it is superfluous. In fine weather, with plenty of dry material on hand, it *is* easy to make a fire, but it's one thing to make a fire and another to make one properly, while not a little skill and experience are required to kindle a blaze when everything is soaking wet, soggy with moisture and the wind is blowing a gale, and rain is driving down in torrents.

Moreover, matches are valuble when camping out, and every camper should know how to build a fire in any weather without wasting a single match. The size of the fire you build must depend very largely upon the weather, the type of camp you use and the purposes for which you are to use it. Indians, as a rule, build a very small fire and tend it constantly, while white woodsmen usually make a roaring fire and trust to the coals keeping up sufficient heat to warm the camp over night and to start a new fire in the morning, and little attention is required save to throw on a log now and then. In the one case, one gets little sleep and must huddle over and nurse the tiny blaze, while in the other a vast amount of fuel is wasted, and one roasts while the fire is blazing and shivers after it dies down. It is far better to build a medium-sized fire and after a short time you will learn to wake up and replenish the fire at regular intervals.

Many campers use one fire both for heating the camp and for cooking, and if you use a tepee, with a fire inside, this is all very well, but in case your fire is in the open, as is necessary with a lean-to or shack, it is a better plan to build two fires, one for heating purposes and the other for cooking.

In any event, the method of starting the fire is the same and with one fire going you can easily kindle as many more as you like.

The first important item in building a fire is to have an abundance of the proper materials ready to your hand. When your fuel is ready, gather a number of light, dry chips and twigs and the dry, resinous branches of evergreens, such as the dead stubs which may always be found sticking out from evergreen trees, and, if there are white birches in the neighbourhood, secure a quantity of the bark. Birch bark is a very useful thing, for it will burn readily, even when damp or green, and every camper should carry a roll of bark with him for use in emergencies.

Make a little criss-cross pile of the driest kindlings and shreds of bark, and right here let me caution you against splitting up or breaking the dry sticks until you are ready to use them. A dead stick may be soaking wet externally and yet dry and inflammable inside, and if it is split open at the last minute it will catch fire readily, whereas, five minutes' exposure to fog, dew, rain or damp air may make it so soggy it is worthless as kindling.

There is quite a little knack in arranging the kindlings so as to blaze up quickly and surely at the first attempt. The best way is to build a little pile, like a miniature log cabin, and over this place dry sticks in conical form like a little tepee. Then light a bit of birch bark, or a resinous twig, thrust it under the kindlings and nurse the tiny blaze until it burns briskly. Do not smother it with too much fuel, and don't wait until the kindlings have burned away to coals before adding more fuel; but keep adding twigs, bark, and chips, little by little, and increasing the size of the sticks as the blaze gains in size, until a good lively fire is burning.

As soon as you have the fire well under way, place a good sized green, hardwood log on each side of the fire and as far apart as is convenient for resting pots, pans or other cooking utensils across the logs. These side logs should be of hickory, maple, oak or some similar slow burning wood, for they are not intended to serve as fuel, but as resting places for your cooking utensils and as backlogs to confine the fire within certain limits.

If the fire is to be used only for cooking, the logs may be two or three feet in length and about six inches in diameter, while for a large heating fire, they should be at least eight feet long and fully eight inches in diameter.

If one fire is to be used for both cooking and heating, the logs should be placed close together at one end and wider apart at the other, to form a "*V*," and the cooking utensils may then be placed across the narrow space over a bed of coals raked from the main fire, between the ends of the logs farther apart.

For the heating fire, place two or three logs outside of the first two, and then, as the latter become charred and burned away, the others may be rolled forward to take their places. The heating fire for a lean-to should be fed with sticks several inches in diameter and three or four feet in length, for smaller sticks throw little heat, although they burn brightly. Such a fire, placed six or eight feet distant from the front of a lean-to, will throw enough heat inside the camp to keep it comfortably warm, even on cold winter nights.

As long as the fire is fed and kept blazing, there will be no trouble about keeping warm, and when ready to turn in for the night, two or three heavy hardwood logs, thrown on the coals, will smoulder and burn all night. Even if they die down and do not blaze, they will still give out considerable heat. Whenever one of the campers wakes up he should stir the fire, turn the logs over and perhaps throw on a new log, and in this way a uniform moderate fire may be kept burning all through the night with little trouble.

In order to build a fire intelligently, or to keep the fire going to the best advantage with the least waste of fuel, every camper should be familiar with the properties of wood in his vicinity. It is a common mistake for amateurs to look upon all kinds of timber as equally suitable for fuel, but, as a matter of fact, every wood has peculiarities of its own, and the wood which will give the best results for one purpose may be very unsuitable for another. By knowing the woods a great deal of trouble, annoyance and uncertainty may be avoided, and you should strive to familiarise yourself with the woods within reach of your camp and select them with regard to the purposes for which they are to be employed.

As examples of this, beech, oak, maple, chestnut and hickory are all good firewoods, while elm, hemlock, spruce and fir are poor; but each of these has properties of which the skilled camper may take advantage. Thus, chestnut does not make a lasting fire, but gives out a good heat and produces fine coals for cooking purposes; hickory does not blaze freely, but makes splendid beds of coals and lasts a long time, but is liable to die out unless mixed with lighter woods; beech and maple are both good heating woods and burn well, while birch gives a good heat, blazes freely, makes good coals and is the best wood for all around use, as it will burn when green or wet; but it has the disadvantage of burning too rapidly for a lasting night fire and should be mixed with hickory or other heavy, slow-burning woods. Elm burns poorly and it smoulders and smokes; pine blazes freely, but it gives little heat and it smokes, while hemlock, spruce and fir blaze well, but snap and crackle, and throw dangerous showers of sparks.

After a long rain, or in a heavy shaded woods, it is often very difficult even for an expert woodsman to light a fire, and if you wish to avoid long delays and loss of patience and temper, you should always be provided with a few dry resinous twigs and strips of birch bark, or similar kindlings, kept in a waterproof box or package. An Indian, or a veteran woodsman, can almost always find dry material, but it is far quicker and easier to carry a supply at all times.

If you have no dry fuel on hand, and the woods are sopping, you should know where to search for dry materials with which to start a fire. Dead trees, especially balsam fir, hemlock, pine, cedar, cottonwood, etc., usually contain dry wood in the centre, and oftentimes the under side of a dead and fallen tree or a log or a branch will be found dry and inflammable if it has been kept off the ground by stones or other logs. In the shelter of large fallen trees, and under overhanging ledges and in small cavities among rocks, one may often find dry leaves, twigs and similar material, while squirrels' nests, either in hollow trees or among the branches, often provide a good supply of shredded cedar bark, twigs, dried leaves and nut shells.

Although there is little excuse for finding one-self in the woods without an ample supply of matches, yet accidents will happen and matches may become wet or damp and useless. To guard against such misfortunes, a flint and steel lighter, or a patent cigar lighter, should always be included in every camping outfit. But even these may be lost or useless, and any one who spends much time in the woods, or goes far from civilisation on a camping trip, should know how to make fire without matches.

If provided with a flint and steel, this is comparatively easy, and in most parts of the world one may find a quantity of pebbles which, if struck with the back of a knife or an axe, will produce sparks capable of igniting tinder.

If you use a regular flint and steel, such as are sold for lighting cigars, you will find little difficulty in striking a spark, for the prepared cotton tinder ignites readily, after it has once been charred; but if you resort to a makeshift of pebble and knife you will find it absolutely impossible to obtain fire unless you have the right kind of punk or tinder to catch the sparks.

Dry cedar bark, dry and rotten pine and spruce twigs, dried moss and lichens, resinous pine or balsam, dry sawdust and many other common things may be used at a pinch, but the best of all materials to be found in the woods are dried "puff balls" or other fungus growths. Far better than any natural substance, however, is a bit of charred cotton rope or twisted cotton rag.

To obtain a fire with flint and steel requires a little knack, but it is an art easily mastered. Hold the punk or tinder against the under side of the flint or pebble and strike the steel sharply down across the edge of the stone (*Fig. 2*). A shower of bright sparks will fly from the pebble and, after two or three attempts, one or more of the sparks will lodge on the tinder, which will commence to smoulder and glow. As soon as this occurs, blow upon it until a good-sized red spot appears, and then, by placing bits of fine dry shavings, sawdust and cedar bark, or similar inflammable materials, upon the glowing punk, and blowing or fanning it, a blaze will soon spring up. It must be admitted, however, that it is much more difficult to kindle a fire in this way than it sounds; but with a little patience and practice, you will be able to accomplish the feat every time, and the knack, once acquired, is never forgotten, and, as it is a most useful and valuable accomplishment, much time may profitably be spent in learning the trick.

Fig 1

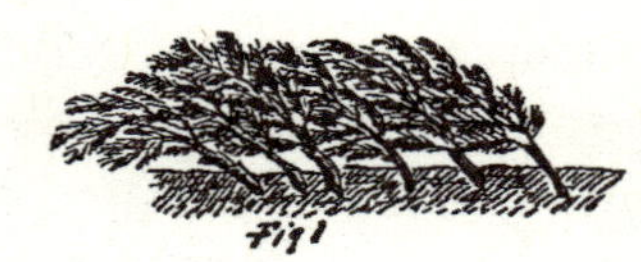

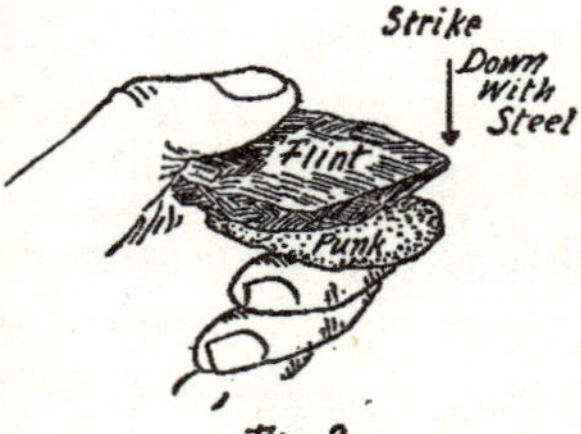

Fig. 2

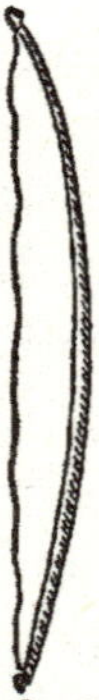

Fig. 3

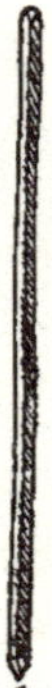

Fig. 4

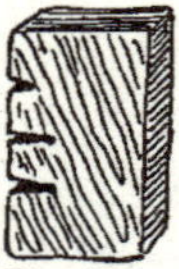

Fig. 5

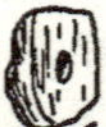

Fig. 6

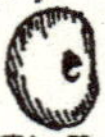

Fig. 7

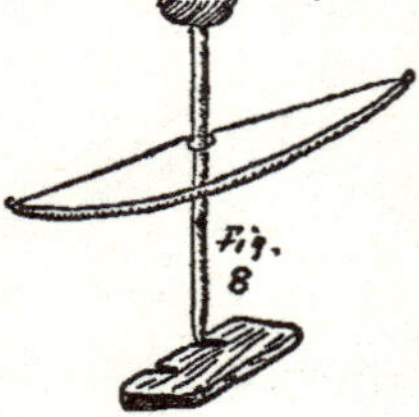

Fig. 8

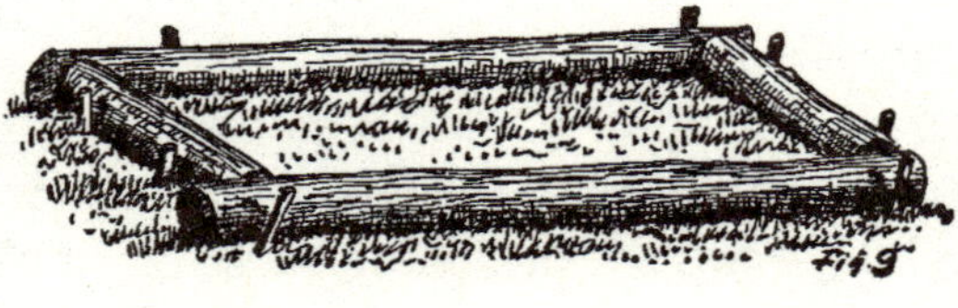

Fig 9

Even without matches or flint or steel, a fire may be kindled by means of bow and drill, which is an adaptation of the more primitive method of rubbing two sticks together.

It must not be supposed that his is a simple matter for the beginner, however, for a good deal of practice and patience are required; but the real success or failure in making fire by this simple method depends upon having exactly the right sort of materials. As these cannot always be secured readily, it is a good plan for the camper to carry a bow and drill outfit with him and to practise its use, especially if going far from civilisation, where there is danger of losing or exhausting one's supply of matches.

The appliances required for making a fire by bow and drill are as follows: The Bow (*Fig. 3*). This is a curved stiff stick about 25 inches long and from ½ to ¾ of an inch in diameter, and with a leather string (an old shoe lace will answer). The string should not be tight, like a real bowstring, but should have enough slack so that a turn may be taken around the drill.

The Drill (*Fig. 4*) is a six- or eight-sided stick, from 12 to 18 inches long and ¾ inch in diameter, pointed at one end and smoothly rounded off at the other.

The Fire Block (*Fig. 5*). This is a flat piece of very dry wood about ¾ of an inch thick and of almost any size, with notches cut on one edge.

The Drill Socket (*Fig. 6-7*). This may be a

knot of wood, a piece of bark or a pebble with a small hole or recess in one side.

The Tinder. Shredded dry cedar bark, dried fungus or moss or any good tinder, as described for use with flint and steel.

Fully as important as the tools are the materials from which they are made. Balsam fir, hemlock, cedar, hickory or any strong light wood will serve for the bow. The drill *must* be of old thoroughly dry but *not* rotten or punky wood, and the best woods for the purpose are fir, cottonwood, basswood, cedar, larch, pine or sagebrush. But of all materials for a drill, cottonwood roots are the best. The fire block should be made from dry fir, pine, hemlock, or some similar soft, free-burning wood.

To secure fire with the bow and drill place a piece of dry pine punk on the ground, place the fire block on this and hold it in position with one foot. With the string of the bow, take a turn around the drill (*Fig. 8*), and place the pointed end of the drill in a notch in the fire block. Hold the drill socket in the left hand and rest it firmly on the upper, rounded end of the drill, thus holding the latter upright. Grasp the bow in the right hand and with steady, long strokes, draw the bow back and forth, thus revolving the drill in its socket. After a few moments a brownish wood powder will accumulate on the punk below the fire block, while the notch in the block will increase in size and a wisp of smoke will rise from it. As soon as this occurs, press more firmly on the drill and work the bow more rapidly. Presently the powdery wood dust will smoke and become charred, when the bow should at once be cast aside and the heap of smouldering dust should be fanned or blown gently until it smokes freely. Then lift off the fire block and place bits of finely-shredded bark or other tinder in the pile of dust, place another piece of dry pine punk over the powder and tinder, and grasping both pieces of wood, with the powder between them, wave the whole in the air or blow upon it until it flames.

Of course, if you are tramping or travelling about and making camp only at night or for short stops, you will not require any camp furnishings save the beds of fir boughs. And here let me suggest that if you are travelling by canoe or boat, by automobile or by any conveyance, you will find a good hammock a most satisfactory sleeping arrangement. Not a fancy lawn or porch hammock or a heavy canvas affair, but a light South American hammock of fibre or cotton.

Don't have the hammock too small,—it should be at least ten feet long and five or six feet wide when spread open,—and don't hang it too loosely, so that you will double up like a half-open knife when resting in it. Hang it as nearly horizontally as possible, and, to sleep well and comfortably in it, lie diagonally across it.

But to return to camp furniture. If in a camp for some time, or in a permanent camp, simple furnishings will prove a great convenience and, moreover, the construction of tables, beds, chairs and other objects will prove a pleasurable and interesting way of spending your spare time.

An improvement over the ordinary bed of balsam or hemlock fans may be made by arranging four logs,—two about eight feet long and the other two about four feet long,—in the form of a rectangle and secured in position by means of stakes as in *Fig. 9*.

The space thus enclosed may be filled with the fir fans, as already described; but with the logs confining the fans, fairly large boughs may be used for the first layer and more layers of fans may be thatched in, thus forming a much softer and thicker bed.

A still better bed is the Willow Bed, such as is used by many of the Western Indians. For making this, you should secure about 60 or 70 straight sticks about the diameter of a lead pencil and 30 inches in length, and in addition to these you should have three or four stouter rods, about half an inch in diameter. Preferably all of these should be of willow, but any other strong elastic wood will answer. Having secured the rods, cut notches or grooves about half an inch from each end of every stick. In addition to the rods you will require a quantity of strong cord or light rope about ⅛ inch in diameter; a ball or spool of strong linen thread or fine twine, and a piece of shoemaker's wax. From the cord, cut four pieces each twenty feet in length, and in the centre of each piece tie a loop, as in *Fig. 10 A*.

Select a couple of trees about 8 feet apart, and in each of these drive four nails or pegs, nine and one-half inches apart, as in *Fig. 10 B*.

Over the pegs or nails in one tree, slip the loops in the cords and twist the free ends tightly together, being sure to twist *against* the lay or twist of the cord, so that the tendency of the cord will be to stay twisted, and having done this, tie the ends of each cord around the proper nail in the second tree, as in *Fig. 10 C.*

Next open the twisted strands of the cords and slip one of the stout sticks through the openings

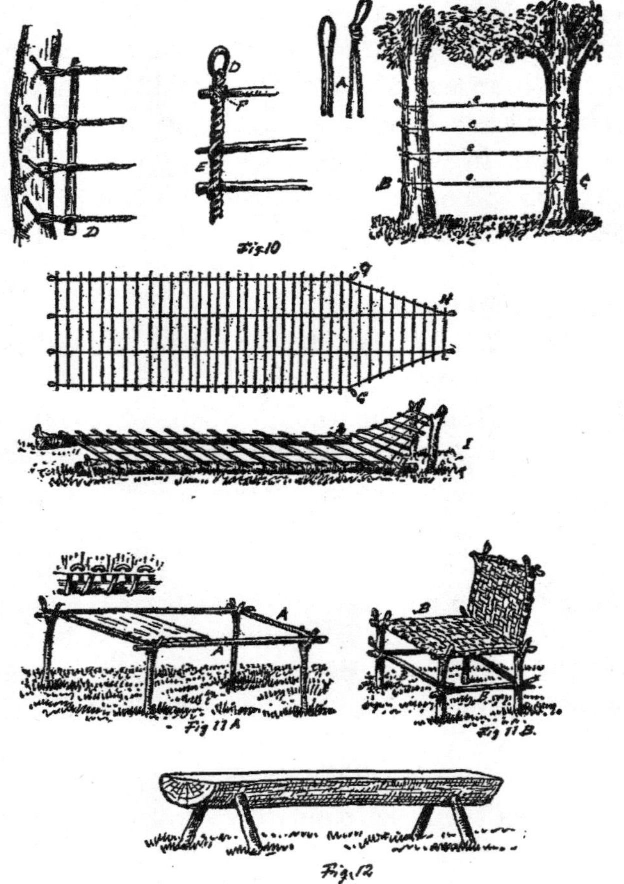

Fig 10

Fig 11 A.

Fig 11 B.

Fig. 12

and push it up close against the loop knot, as in *Fig. 10 D.*

Then insert one of the smaller rods in the same way, leaving an inch of cord between it and the first rod, and being careful to place the butt or larger end of one rod next to the smaller end of the one before it (*Fig. 10 E*).

Proceed in this way with the rods and at each spot where a rod passes through a twisted cord lash cord and rod together firmly with the waxed thread, as in *Fig. 10 F.* Continue in this manner for a distance of six feet, and then insert another stout rod and make loops in the two outer cords, as shown in *Fig. 10 G.*

From this point, decrease the length of the rods as you proceed, thus narrowing down the bed for a length of 18 inches, as in *Fig. 10 H,* and use a stout rod for the last.

The bed is now completed by tying and lashing loops in the ends of the two outer cords, close to the last rod, and the whole may then be removed from the pegs or nails. The bed may be set up for use by placing it on a frame of logs and staking out the corners, as in *Fig. 10 I,* or, if desired, it may be covered with canvas, blankets or balsam fans. If the latter are used, the butts should be inserted through the spaces between the rods, and each layer should overlap the one preceding, exactly as in making an ordinary fir-fan bed. If the bed is made with large cord and rather large rods at the ends, it may be slung like a hammock. Such a bed will be found very springy and comfortable, and as it can be rolled up into a compact bundle and is very light, it may easily be transported from camp to camp.

In case no suitable trees can be found, a frame for making the bed may be built by driving a couple of stakes in the earth, or the cords may be attached to a bough, pole or beam overhead, and their lower ends kept tight by being attached to another pole or log suspended a few inches from the earth.

Tables may also be made very easily by driving forked sticks into the earth and then lashing a rectangular frame to them, and which should then be covered by birch bark as in *Fig. 11 A.*   In place of the bark, rods or withes may be lashed close together, or cords may be stretched across the top and wattled with willow, withes, or other materials.   Chairs or benches may be constructed in the same manner, with legs lashed to the corners and braces fastened from leg to leg, as in *Fig. 11 B,* or if they are to remain in one place, as is the case of benches about a table or in camp, the chairs may be made by wattling a frame fastened between upright stakes.

Another method of making a rough and ready seat or bench is to hew off one side of a log until smooth and flat, bore four holes in the rounded side, and in these drive stout sticks to serve as legs (*Fig. 12*).

Of course, if you have hammers, saws, nails and other tools with you, it is a very simple matter to construct all sorts of rustic furniture, but those mentioned may all be made with material found in the woods, and with no tools other than a knife, an axe and a ball of twine. The last is not really essential, for roots, strips of bark, vines or twisted withes will serve as well as cord for lashings.

If you require hooks, on which to hang clothing, cooking utensils or any other articles, it is only necessary to cut down a young well-branched sapling and trim off the branches a few inches from the trunk. This may be suspended from the tent rope or shack rafters, or driven into the earth, and will make a very useful rack on which any articles may be hung out of the way and safe from dampness or ants.

A very important part of camping out is camp housekeeping, and the camper should strive to keep his woodland home as clean, neat and tidy as the most particular housewife. Far too many campers pay little or no heed to such matters, and many camps are slovenly, littered and disgracefully dirty. Nothing looks worse, and nothing disgusts the true woodsman and nature lover more, than to find a camp site littered with odds and ends of tin cans, papers, empty bottles and other rubbish, and there is no earthly excuse for such a state of affairs. Within a short distance of the camp, a good-sized hole should be dug, as soon as camp is made, and into this all refuse should be thrown. Before leaving the spot, the hole should be filled with earth, and if you are staying in the camp for several days or longer, a layer of earth should be scattered over the refuse each day, in order to prevent flies and insects from being attracted and also to avoid any unpleasant odours.

Never throw refuse of any sort into ponds, lakes or streams. It is not only unsightly, but contaminates the water and may cause illness or even death to others who drink the water, thinking it unpolluted.

Keep everything orderly and have a place for every article, and make it a point to keep everything in its place.   A skilled woodsman should be able to place his hand unerringly on any desired article in the darkest night, and if you acquire the habit of mislaying or leaving things here, there and everywhere, you'll either lose something or will waste valuable time, and your temper, trying to find articles in a hurry.   Cleanliness, too, is very important in camp. Because there's plenty of clean air and pure water, and unlimited space, is no excuse for keeping a dirty camp, and it's far easier to clean everything up at regular times than to let things go until sheer necessity compels you to do a week's cleaning at one time.

Amateur campers are too prone to lay aside dishes and cooking utensils unwashed and put off cleaning them until required for the next meal. Washing dishes is an unpleasant job at best, and in camp there is always a tendency to avoid this work, but, like a great many other unpleasant tasks, it's easier to get it over with at once than to put it off and have it constantly on your mind as a bugbear.

With a fire going, there is no reason for not having a supply of hot water for washing dishes and clothes, and if the pot is placed on the coals when the meal is served, the water will be hot and ready to use by the time the meal is over. But even without hot water, it is easy to keep dishes clean and metal cooking utensils bright and shining. By scrubbing them in a brook or lake, and using a handful of moss and sand, or a bit of sod, for a dish rag, the dishes and pots and pans may be kept as free from dirt and grease as by means of soap and patent cleansers.

It is particularly necessary to keep cooking utensils perfectly clean, for cooking over wood smokes and soots the pots or pans, and if this is not removed at once it becomes baked and burned on until it is next to impossible to clean off the nasty blackness. Then, when the utensils are stowed in the pack or duffle-bag, the soot is transferred to the canvas and will be smudged onto clothing and everything else which touches it.

If several are camping together, it is an easy matter to divide the various duties of camp housekeeping, so that each member of the party takes turns at the chores. As a rule, however, one member of the party usually excels at cooking, and you will fare better if the position of cook is held constantly by the one most skilled in culinary arts. But, in return, the cook should be exempted from all other duties, save in the case of emergency, and he should not be expected to wash dishes, cut firewood, build camp, lug water or do anything save to prepare the meals and enjoy himself between times.

If every member of a camping party has his special duties each day, and takes turns with the others, there will be no cause for complaint, each will be doing his share, and no one will feel that he is a drudge of the others, which is one of the commonest causes of dissension in camping parties.

Finally, and very important, is the matter of cooking in camp. Many a person who can cook at home in a well-appointed kitchen and with a coal fire in a range, will fail utterly when in the woods with only a saucepan and an open wood fire at his disposal. Never start on a camping trip without some member who is a good hand at simple out of doors cooking, and if there is no such member of the party, be sure to take a few lessons from mother, sister or hired cook, and do a little practising at home before you start for the woods.

Don't try to prepare elaborate meals or be too anxious to exhibit your skill in camp. The simpler the meals, the better, and a few well-made flapjacks, a bit of broiled bacon, some fish or game, and a steaming aromatic cup of coffee, is a far more sustaining and satisfactory meal than a soggy dumpling and highly flavoured sauces. One always has a good appetite when camping, and an abundance of nutritious, simple, well cooked food is the most welcome fare.

It is a difficult matter to describe how to cook, but the following brief hints may serve to give you ideas as to the resources of camp cookery and may be of help to those who have but little knowledge of cooking with limited supplies and conveniences.

The simplest of all things to cook are fish and game, and while any one can broil or roast a piece of meat over the coals, some little knowledge is required in order to make such food really palatable and tasty.

Nearly all four-footed game should be skinned and dressed as soon after being killed as possible, and, as a rule, all animals should be hung in the shade for several days after being dressed and before being cooked. In very hot weather care should be taken that the meat is not tainted or fly-blown, and small game should be eaten within a few hours after being killed, but great care should be taken that no game or meat of any description is cooked until after all animal heat has disappeared, as otherwise serious illness may result.

Birds should be plucked and drawn as soon as convenient after being killed, and may be eaten as soon as animal heat has all disappeared, or, if preferred, they may be kept for a day or two, while fish should invariably be cooked as soon after being taken from the water as is possible.

The South American Indians have a method of preserving game fresh and free from flies for many days, and which is known as "Bucanning." It is a very simple method and should be more widely known and used by campers and dwellers in the woods. After being cleaned and skinned, or plucked, the game is suspended over a smoky fire until thoroughly smoked and slightly cooked on the outside. It is then laid aside and may be cooked at any time, as required. I have eaten game thus bucanned after being kept for two weeks in the hot tropical forests of Guiana, and yet the meat was as fresh, juicy and well flavoured as if freshly killed.

The simplest method of cooking game is by broiling, and there are few methods of cooking game which give a better flavour, if properly done. But simple as it seems, many a broiled piece of meat is rendered unpalatable and indigestible by improper cooking, and a few words as to broiling may not be amiss.

To broil a squirrel, rabbit or other small animal, first skin and dress carefully and remove all bruised or discoloured flesh and blood clots. Cut off and throw aside the head and feet, and split the body into two parts by cutting longitudinally along the backbone. Spit each piece on a hardwood stick and broil over coals until slightly seared on both sides. Sprinkle with salt and pepper and cook slowly over the coals until done, being careful to turn frequently to insure even cooking.

To broil birds, pick as usual, split open along back and remove entrails, sprinkle with salt and pepper and broil slowly over coals.

Grouse or other large birds may be broiled by the same method, but a slice of bacon or pork, skewered to the upper side, will add greatly to the juiciness and flavour. If the bird is very large, or you are in a hurry, slice pieces from the breast, disjoint the legs and wings, and spit these on a stick with a slice of pork or bacon between each piece and broil as usual.

Slices of venison or beef may be broiled in the same way.

To broil fish, scale and clean. Split down the back; flatten out and broil on a grid of green sticks or iron over a bed of coals. Before placing on an iron grid, the latter should be well greased. By placing strips of bacon or pork over the fish, a better flavour will be obtained. In the case of small fish, the heads should be left on and the fish broiled on the end of a green stick, like small animals. After the fish are broiled, sprinkle with salt and pepper and spread with butter or fat and hold over the fire until the latter is melted.

Frying Game Birds and Animals. To prepare birds or small animals for frying, cut them into medium sized pieces, parboil until tender (in the case of old or tough birds), sprinkle with salt and pepper, roll in flour and fry in melted pork fat or bacon. To make gravy, save the grease in the pan, stir in half a cup of flour until the frying fat turns a rich brown, add a little of the water in which the game was parboiled, bring to a boil, while stirring constantly, and season with pepper and salt.

Fish should be fried by rolling in flour and frying in very hot fat.

Game Fricasseed. Pluck or skin and dress as usual and cut into pieces of convenient size. Parboil in enough water to cover and, when tender, remove from the pot and drain. Place a few pieces of pork or bacon in the frying pan, until browned slightly. Season with pepper and salt; sprinkle with flour and fry in the pork fat until rich brown. Make a thick gravy of the parboiling water, fat and flour, as already described; add this to the pieces of meat and bring all to a boil. Vegetables may be added if desired.

Fish Chowder. Cut the fish into convenient sized pieces and remove as many of the bones as possible. Slice and fry a quantity of pork fat, (about ¾ pound to each 5 pounds of fish), and fry until partly browned. Have about a dozen potatoes pared and sliced, and fry two medium-sized onions in the fat. Place a layer of the fish in a good-sized pot and on this place a layer of sliced potatoes, then some fried onions, and season with salt and pepper, and add a sprinkling of flour. Then place a few slices of pork or bacon over all, and repeat the alternate layers of fish, potatoes, onions and pork until all have been used. Over all, pour the fat from the frying pan, cover with boiling water, and cook for half an hour or more, according to the quantity of fish and potatoes used. A few minutes before serving, break up stale bread or hard biscuits, dip them in cold water, add them to the pot of chowder, and pour in about a pint of hot milk.

Chicken Chowder may easily be made from canned boneless chicken by placing the contents of the tin in water, adding sliced potatoes, onions and other vegetables, with broken biscuit or crackers if desired, seasoning with pepper and salt and boiling until the potatoes are cooked.

Stewing Rabbits, Birds, or Small Game. Skin or pluck and dress as usual; cut into small pieces and place in a pot. Cover with water, add rice, vegetables and one or two soup tablets or bouillon cubes, season with pepper and salt, and boil until the meat is tender.

Muskrats are excellent food and are extensively eaten in the Southern States. Skin carefully and remove the musk glands, near the root of the tail, without breaking them. Clean well and place in cold water. Bring to a boil for a few minutes, strain off water and fry, broil, or roast, as desired.

Turtles are all edible, with the exception of the musk turtle, and even the wood tortoises are toothsome, although there is little meat on them. First kill the turtles, by plunging in boiling water, and as soon as dead remove and allow to cool. Lay the turtle on its back and, with an axe, hatchet, machete or stout knife, cut the joint where the two shells join. Pull off the lower shell, remove entrails and gall bladder, cut off head and skin the legs and remove toes and outer surface of shell, which will be loosened by the hot water. Place the turtle in a pot of fresh hot water and boil until the meat comes away from the bones. Remove bones and add vegetables, seasoning, etc., and boil until the vegetables are cooked.

An excellent way to bake fish, birds or small game is to roast them in clay. Dress the game without skinning or plucking, enclose the bird or animal in a thick layer of clay and place the whole in the midst of a bed of hot coals. Cover over with more coals, and in about an hour rake out the clay, which will be baked hard. Break this open and the feathers or fur will come away with the clay and will leave the meat beautifully cooked. This is an excellent method for cooking porcupines, whose spines are very troublesome if one attempts to skin the prickly creatures.

Vegetables are easy to cook, and to prepare dried vegetables is a very simple matter, for all that is necessary is to place them in boiling water, stir and add seasoning. Fresh vegetables should be boiled until thoroughly cooked, and to save time they should be placed in plain cold water, as a large portion of the cooking will be accomplished while the water is coming to a boil. Dried potatoes make excellent griddle cakes. After being thoroughly cooked, mash with a fork or flattened stick until a smooth paste is obtained. Mix this with flour, moisten well, until a tenacious mass is obtained, pat into cakes, sprinkle with dry flour, and fry in a pan with bacon fat, butter or other grease.

Flapjacks are one of the old stand-bys of camp cuisine, and every camper should know how to make them. To two pints of flour, add two heaping teaspoonfuls of baking powder, one level teaspoonful of salt, two or three spoonfuls of dried egg, and mix thoroughly while dry. Add six heaping dessertspoonfuls of evaporated milk and water (or an equivalent amount of dry milk or fresh milk), add water slowly, while mixing, until a smooth, uniform thick batter results. The batter should be thin enough to drip or run freely from a spoon, but not too thin or watery. Fry in a pan greased with fat or lard. You will find it easier to fry small cakes at first, as these may easily be turned with a broad bladed knife, but after a little practise, you will be able to make cakes the full size of the bottom of the pan and to turn them over by a twist of the pan. When you can toss a flapjack a foot or two in the air and catch it, other side up, on the pan, you can consider yourself a true camp cook. The only difficulty in making flapjacks is in mixing the batter to the proper consistency. If too thin, it will make brittle, tough cakes, and if too thick, it will be difficult to cook the centre before the outer surfaces are scorched. The best method, until you are sure of the proportions, is to make a thick batter and add water gradually until the right consistency is obtained, as it is easier to thin the batter than to thicken it.

Another strictly camp dish is known as *Dope*, and is prepared as follows: Cut about a pound of salt pork into small dice-shaped pieces, place them on the pan with a little water and boil for one minute. Pour off the water and fry the pork until slightly browned. Remove the pieces of pork and into the hot fat rub three or four spoonfuls of flour, with pepper and salt to season, and cook the flour without allowing it to brown or scorch. When perfectly smooth and free from lumps, add a quart of water, in which 12 dessertspoonfuls of evaporated milk, or an equal amount of dried milk, has been dissolved (or use half and

half water and fresh milk). Bring this to a boil
slowly, stir constantly, add the pork and serve.
This is probably the best of all methods of serving
pork, and it is also good when used for a sauce
or gravy, while at a pinch it will serve excellently
in place of butter, and will prove delicious on hot
griddle cakes in place of syrup.

Corn Bread or Johnny Cake is another simple
and healthy dish for camp use. To one pint of
flour, add one pint of yellow corn meal, two heaping teaspoonfuls of baking powder, one level teaspoonful of salt, two dessertspoonfuls of dried
egg, one teaspoonful of sugar, and cold pork fat or
lard the size of an egg. Mix thoroughly while
dry; add six heaping dessertspoonfuls of evaporated milk, or an equal amount of dried milk, and
add cold water sufficient to form a thick batter,
and stir until thoroughly mixed. Pour into a
greased pan, place the pan on a bed of dull coals
or hot ashes, cover it tightly, and place hot ashes
or coals over it. Bake about 20 minutes, or until
the cake is thoroughly cooked. One or two trials
will serve to give you an idea of how long the pan
should remain in the ashes.

Baked Beans are another most important camp
dish. They are easy to prepare, but they require
a long time to cook and can only be recommended
for permanent camps or when a stop of several
days is made. Wash the beans and parboil until,
when placed upon a spoon and blown upon, the
skins will split open. When boiled to this state,
drain off the water, wash in cold water and drain
again. Now, place beans in the pot for a depth

of two inches, and on them place about a pound of pork and add the rest of the beans. Season with salt and pepper, add a dessertspoonful of sugar, and cover all with warm water. Cover the bean pot with a thin cloth and force the lid tightly in place. For an oven, have a hole about a foot deep and about a foot in diameter in the ground, and in this have a good fire burning for several hours before you wish to bake, and place a number of stones in the fire. When the stones are red hot, scrape out the ashes, coals and stones, place the pot of beans in the hole, cover it over with coals, hot stones and ashes, and finally place earth over all. Leave for 8 to 10 hours, and remove, when beans will be found to be thoroughly cooked. In rainy weather, cover the spot where the pot is buried with a slab of bark.

To Boil Rice seems like a very simple matter, but it requires some practice and skill to cook rice properly. First wash and rinse the rice, drain and place the grain in boiling water, in the proportion of a cup of rice to each 2 quarts of water. Add 2 teaspoonfuls of salt and boil hard for 15 to 30 minutes, stirring frequently and adding more hot water as the water boils away. When done, the rice should be soft and each grain separate. Too long boiling will produce a mushy, sticky mass. When cooked, drain off the water and set the pot near the fire or on the hot ashes for a moment, in order to drive off any water which may remain.

Hasty Pudding or *Corn Meal Mush* is made by stirring corn meal into cold water in the proportion of 1 cup of meal to 1 quart of water, to which ½ teaspoonful of salt should be added. Bring to a boil, while stirring constantly, and boil for fifteen minutes or until thoroughly cooked.

Hasty pudding may be fried, if allowed to cool, when it should be cut into slices, rolled in flour and fried in very hot grease.

Braising. Tough meat of any sort may be greatly improved by braising in a covered pot or saucepan. This method is particularly good for bear meat, round of beef, or venison shoulders or haunches.

Place the meat in the pot with about two inches of water over the bottom and add a bit of bacon or pork. In the case of bear meat, this should be omitted. Put in some chopped onions, herbs, or other seasoning, cover the pot and cook for 15 minutes to each pound of meat. While cooking, sprinkle with salt and pepper and make the gravy by adding a little water to the grease and thickening with flour until the proper consistency is obtained.

To roast properly, build a good fire of hardwood against a rock or a large green backlog. Sear the outside of the roast in the clear flame, skewer on thin slices of pork at one end, and hang the meat closer to the fire by a strong wet string or withe.

Have the slices of pork on the upper side, turn the meat frequently, and place a pan or green bark trough beneath it to catch the drippings. Each time the roast is turned, it should be basted with the drippings.

For broiling, coals should always be used, while for roasting, a hot fire is the best. If you are frying, do not attempt to use a flaming fire or a large bed of coals, as the grease may catch fire. Either make a small fire of dry sticks not thicker than your finger, and feed this from time to time to maintain a steady heat, or else rake a thin layer of coals in front of the fire and add new coals as the bed dies down.

Occasionally you may have so much game or fish that you cannot use all of it at one time, and in such cases you should know how to preserve the supply for future use.

I have already mentioned "bucanning," but there are many other effective ways of keeping meat for a long time.

Venison will keep very well without any preparation, and, in fact, this meat is not really good until it has hung for a long time. If a handful of salt is placed in an incision in a haunch of venison, the meat will keep for weeks. In warm weather, venison may be rubbed with flour, sewn up in a bag of cheesecloth, and hung in a shady spot, and if thus prepared and the bag is tight, the meat will keep for several weeks.

Fish may readily be dried by splitting them along the back, removing backbones and entrails and rubbing the fish with salt, after which they should be hung on a frame over a smoky fire. If a small, conical, tepee-like bark structure is made and a fire built within it, the fish may be thoroughly smoked by suspending them within the tepee for three or four days.

PART II
TRAILING AND TRAMPING

CHAPTER IV

TRAILS. BLAZING A WAY. SIGNALLING. DIRECTION AND DISTANCE. MEASURING HEIGHTS AND DISTANCES.

ONE may camp out for years and never acquire a knowledge of woodcraft if hired guides or woodsmen are employed, but one never knows when a knowledge of woodcraft, of trailing, or of similar matters, may be necessary. It is an easy method to depend upon one's guides and never give a thought to the mysteries of woodcraft, but it is much wiser to be able to depend upon yourself and to feel confident that you can follow a trail, find your way or eke out a living in the woods without any one to aid you, and every camper should strive to become as skilled in woodcraft as the professional guide.

Not only is such a knowledge valuable and important as a safeguard, but in addition the pleasures of out of door life are greatly enhanced if the camper is a good woodsman, able to follow

a trail, to find his way or to travel through the forest by nature's signs, and to convey his wishes and directions by means of signals from a distance; in short, to feel no fear or hesitation about going anywhere in the wilderness without danger of going astray or of suffering from want.

The question of becoming lost is a very grave one, even in fairly small areas of forest, and many a camper loses much of the enjoyment of his stay in the woods through fear of going astray if he wanders out of sight of camp.

The first thing every camper should learn in regard to woodcraft is to follow a trail. In our northern forests, trails or routes are usually indicated by marks or "blazes" cut on the trees, and while these may prove meaningless and confusing to the novice, yet they are very easy to understand and convey a clear story to the woodsman. Indeed, we often speak of a person "leaving a blazed trail behind him," when we wish to convey the idea that his footsteps are easy to follow, and for the same reason, we hear of explorers and pioneers "blazing a way for civilisation."

Almost any one can follow a blazed trail by looking for the spots or blazes on the trees, but it is quite a different matter for one to "read" the trail and proceed accordingly, for there are numerous forms of these marks, and each form, as well as its position, has a definite meaning. Once these meanings are learned, one can follow any trail as easily and surely as if the way were marked by signposts, for the blazes, like pigeon-English, is a "lingua franca" of the woods, and is understood by all versed in woodcraft.

As with every other rule, there are exceptions to this, however, and quite frequently one may come upon blazes which convey no meaning whatever, even to the experienced woodsman. But these are usually of no real value or importance, for they are merely private marks, indicating some particular location, trap or other item of interest only to the maker or his companions.

All regular blazes may be classed under three general heads: the first consisting of a single mark or blaze; the second of two blazes side by side, and the third, of three or more marks, one over another. The first is the ordinary everyday trail mark, used to denote the path or trail; the second shows turns or direction, and the last warns of danger, or spots where caution is necessary before proceeding.

These three classes of blazes are illustrated in *Figs. 1, 2, 3, 4.* In *Fig. 1,* the single mark or trail blaze is shown. Such a mark means that you should proceed straight ahead to the next mark. When such a blaze as in *Fig. 2* is seen, you should turn to the right and look about for the next single mark, while if you come to the mark shown in *Fig. 3,* a turn to the left should be made. Three spots in perpendicular line, as in *Fig. 4,* show that danger is near, and you should move carefully. It may be a bad windfall, a hidden hole or gorge, a trap, or any other danger, and as long as the three marks are in sight, go forward slowly and cautiously until the regular single marks again appear. Sometimes the position of the danger is indicated by a mark at one side, but in any case the three marks are equivalent to a red flag or a red light, and call for caution.

In addition to these three simple forms of blazes, there are various combinations in which two or more are used, as illustrated in *Figs. 5, 6,*

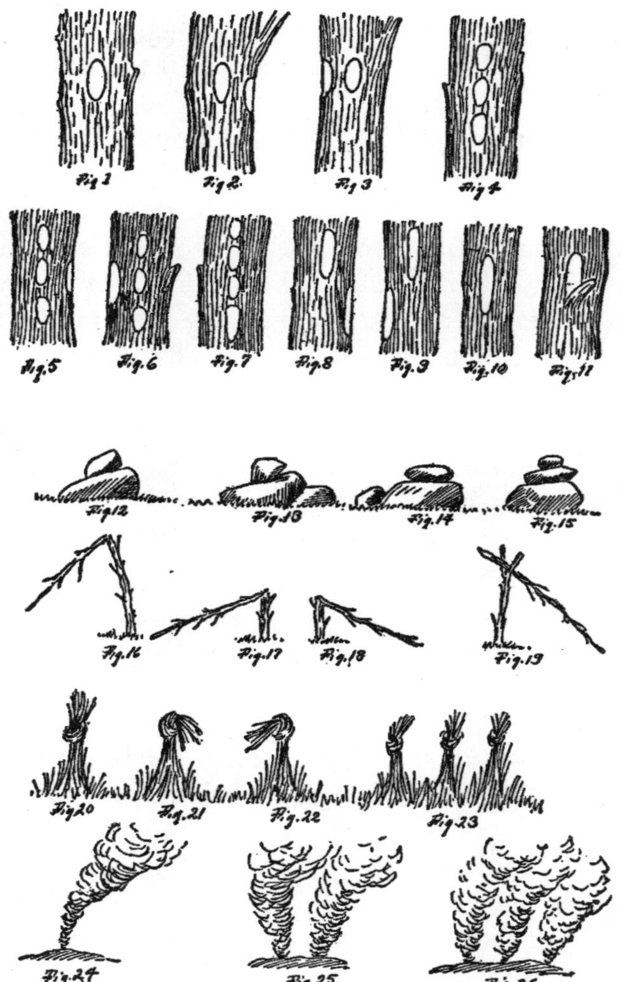

7.   Thus, in *Fig. 5*, the blazes indicate that danger lurks to the right, and hence you should pass to the left, while *Fig. 6* shows a danger at left, and consequently you should turn to the right. *Fig. 7*, however, indicates a survey line, and warns the woodsman not to cut or injure the trees upon which it appears.

Still other combinations are shown in *Figs. 8, 9*.   These are camp marks, as indicated by the long perpendicular blaze, while the marks to right or left and below show whether the camp site lies to right or left of the trail.   Such marks as are shown in *Figs, 10, 11*, are private blazes and of importance only to those who made them, or to those who understand their significance.

When a trail is frequently traversed, the way is kept plain by each passing traveller chopping blazes afresh, and so, on a well-used trail, practically every tree will bear a blaze and one may follow it rapidly and easily.   An old trail, or one which is seldom used, may be very difficult to follow, however, for the blazes become weathered and healed, and it is often very hard to find the marks.

Whenever you go into a strange forest, or when one of the party is straggling behind, you should always blaze a trail for the others to follow.   It is an easy matter to whack off a bit of the trees, as you walk along, and this fresh trail will serve to guide those behind you, as well as to enable you to retrace your steps with ease and certainty.   In case you wish to identify your own trail or to indicate your presence to others, you should make your blazes of distinctive size or form. An old woodsman can recognise the trail marks of all his friends and acquaintances by the form or position of their blazes.

You will soon find that, with a little practise, it is very easy to blaze a good trail, and that it takes little time to do so, as you tramp through the woods, for all you have to do is to chop a bit of bark from the trees, a few rods apart. Don't make the marks either too high or too low, for, in the first case, they are hard to see, and, in the second, they may become concealed by brush, while if made about the height of one's shoulder, they will catch the eye readily.

While blazes are most extensively used in indicating trails through a forested country, it is impossible to mark a trail in this way where trees are scarce or absent. But it is just as easy to indicate a trail or to follow one in such places as it is to make or follow a blazed trail in the woods.

There are several methods of doing this, and the trail in open country may be marked by stones, bent or broken twigs, or wisps or bunches of grass or reeds, as shown in *Figs. 12* to *23*.

But, no matter which method is employed, the same symbols and combinations are used as on a blazed trail. Thus, one stone or another, a single bent or broken branch, or a single tied or twisted bunch of grass, as in *Figs. 12, 16, 20,* shows the straight trail. A stone to right or left of a trail mark, a twig pointing to either side, or a bunch of grass pointed to right or left, as in *Figs. 13, 14, 17, 18, 21, 22,* indicates a turn, while three stones, a separate twig resting on another, or three wisps of grass, means danger or caution. *Figs. 15, 19, 23.*

Much time may profitably be spent in learning to make and read these various trail marks, and until you are sure of your memory and of the meaning of all these symbols, you should carry a slip of paper or a card on which the various marks and their meanings are shown.

Oftentimes you may find yourself in strange woods, where there are no blazed trails and while, by blazing a trail as you proceed, you may be able to retrace your steps, yet this will not enable you to reach your objective point or prevent you from going in a roundabout, erratic manner from one place to another. A compass is a great help, and you should always carry one, but unless you know in which direction you wish to go or the direction in which your objective point lies from your camp, the compass will serve merely to guide you in a straight line and to prevent you from travelling in a circle. If about to trail through a strange country, always strive to secure the bearings of some prominent landmark, such as hills, rivers, mountains, etc., and the really proficient woodsman should instinctively note such landmarks and bear their position in mind as he proceeds.

Moss on trees or rocks often indicates the points of the compass, but this varies a great deal in various places, and it often puzzles an expert to decide on which side of an object the moss is thickest.

Dead or stunted branches on one side of a tree usually indicate the northern side, and by training your eyes to note the little differences between the opposite sides of trees, and many other little details, you will soon find that you can tell which is north and which south, although you cannot easily explain just *how* you know.

If there is a bright sun, a watch may be made to serve as a compass, on a pinch. If the dial is held horizontally, with the hour hand pointing at the sun and so that the shadow of the hour hand is directly under the hand itself, then half the distance between that point and the figure 12 will be south, if before noon, and, counting from left to right, or southward, and if afternoon, counting backward, or from right to left. (*Fig. 27.*) Of course, this is only approximate, and it varies more or less with the season and latitude, but it will serve roughly as a guide, and to denote the points of the compass, and will prevent you from walking in a circle, which is the greatest danger when lost in the woods.

But there is no danger of this happening if you make it a rule to blaze a trail as you proceed, for, by sighting back to the last two or three marks, you can always follow a fairly straight line.

Although blazed trails and similar marks will be found of the utmost value in guiding you through the woods, there are limits to their usefulness, and the messages or signals which may be conveyed by marks on trees, stones, bent twigs or bunches of grass, often fall far short of one's requirements.

Oftentimes it is essential that you should be able to communicate with other members of your party when at a distance, or, in case one of the party is lost, it is of the utmost importance that you should be able to let him know of your position or the position of the camp, or that he should have means of notifying his friends of his plight.

In case of accidents, also, a means of communicating one's position may make all the difference between life and death, while still another valuable use for signalling is when various members of a party separate in search of game, water, camping places, etc. Then any discoveries made by one member of the party may be communicated to the others, and all may be brought together without loss of time or weary hours of tramping unnecessarily.

Among savage peoples, various methods of signalling are employed, and, while some of these are very intricate and complicated, others are very simple, and you will be surprised to find how much information may be conveyed by the simplest codes and methods.

There are various means of signalling, but for long distances fires or smokes are most widely used. In case of bright sunlight or in open country, as well as on high hills, unobstructed by trees, signals are often made by flashes of light, while at comparatively short distances, hats, flags or other objects may be used.

Smokes are particularly useful where the country is wooded or there are no high eminences, and on a calm day a good smoke signal may be seen for an extremely long distance. Fires at night serve the same purpose, while the flash of a mirror or a bright metal surface may be seen for many miles. This is the basis of the heliograph used by the army, and while a real heliograph may easily be made, a pocket mirror will serve all ordinary purposes.

No matter which system is used, the ordinary signals are similar to the symbols described for trail marks. Thus one smoke, fire or flash, indicates location; two smokes, fires or flashes, indicate trouble or the desire for aid, while three smokes, fires or flashes, convey good news or that a hunt or search has been successful. Last of all, are four signals, which are used to summon all members of the party to a common meeting place or to camp.

These are all illustrated in *Figs. 24, 25, 26,* and by adding others, or varying these, or by arranging combinations among the various members of the party, almost any message or even a long conversation, may be carried on. A better way is to use the telegraphic code, and as the standard Morse code has many spaced dots, which are difficult to signal, and as the Continental has none, the latter is by all means the best code to use, as follows:

A . - B - . . . C - . - . D - . . E .
F . . - . G - - . H . . . . I . . J . - - -
K - . - L . - . . M - - N - . O - - -
P . - - . Q - - . - R . - . S . . . T -
U . . - V . . . - W . - - X - . . - Y - . - -
Z - - . .

DD means a call or "signalling." W W means "answering." F F means "spelling." IMI means "repeat." A A A means "full stop." G means "go on." MG means "wait." RT means "right." FI means "numeral."

If you do not know the code or do not care to learn it you can carry a copy with you and by referring to it you will be able to send or read any message by means of smokes, fires or flashes. In thus signalling, a dot is represented by one flash smoke or fire of about one second's duration, a dash should be two seconds and a space four seconds, while for a full stop, or space between words, a space of six to ten seconds should be allowed. To use the code with a fire, a blanket or coat should be held in front of the fire and by removing this for the proper length of time a dot or dash may be indicated while the fire should be hidden for four to ten seconds according to whether a space between letters or words is desired. Smoke signals are made by building a good fire, covering it with damp wood, leaves or sod until a dense smoke rises, and using a wet blanket, coat or canvas to stop the smoke. If this is quickly removed and replaced various sized puffs of smoke are produced and these indicate the dots and dashes of the code. In the same way a short flash from a mirror indicates a dot and a longer flash a dash while the intervals between show spaces or stops according to their length.

When the signaller is within view of those to whom he is signalling a stick with a flag, and a cap or hat may be used to transmit the code. The stick or flag should be held in one hand and the cap in the other. The stick, board or flag means a dash and the cap means a dot while both arms lowered indicates a space and both arms up means a full stop (*Fig. 28*).

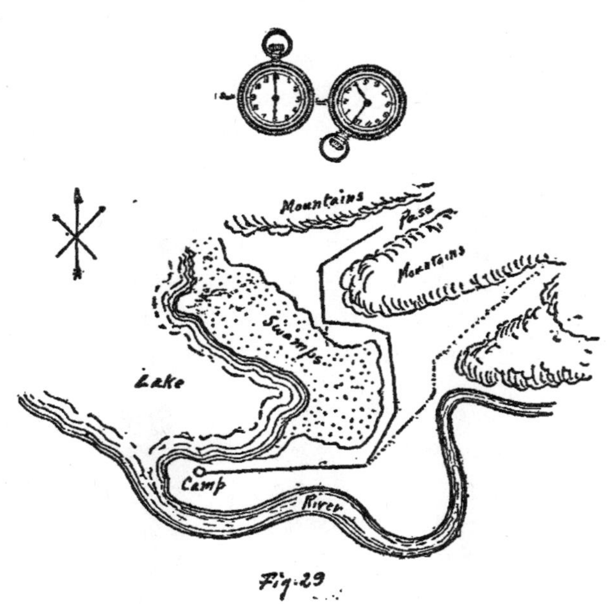

Fig. 29

Still another method is to use two flags of different colours or shapes and, by arranging beforehand which colour or shape means a dot and which a dash, a code may be used which is unintelligible to all save those in the secret.

A very important item in woodcraft is the ability to judge direction and distance. Many people possess a sort of sixth sense by which they unconsciously know the direction in which they are moving, or the relative positions of places, and no matter how often they turn or move about they never become confused or go astray, indeed, it is really a sort of instinct and is absolutely lacking in the majority of people. It is a natural gift to be able to do this, but nearly every one possesses some idea of direction and, if developed by practice and observation, the average person can learn to carry direction and relative positions in his mind to a remarkable degree.

To judge distances accurately is more a matter of practice and judgment than anything else, and many woodsmen are wonderfully expert at this. The average man is a very poor judge of distance, especially in the woods, and no two people will have the same idea of a distance tramped, or of one object from another. Moreover, a man who

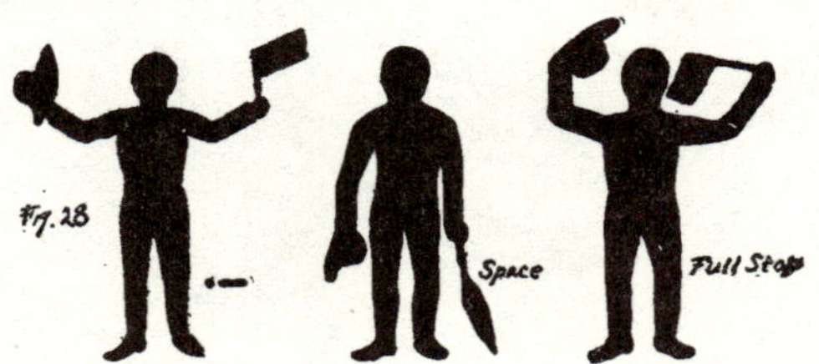

is able to judge distances in one locality, or under certain familiar conditions, may be absolutely at a loss under other conditions or in other places, for the atmospheric conditions, the elevation, the character of the country, the hour of the day and one's own physical condition have much to do with one's ideas of distances. For example, the first time a person walks over a certain trail or route the way invariably seems longer than after the trail becomes familiar and a distance always seems shorter when one is fresh than when one is tired or hungry. So too, in rough or hilly country, or in heavy woods, a ten mile tramp may seem twenty miles or more, while, if one is hunting or interested in the surroundings, a long distance may seem very short. In hazy weather objects appear further away than in clear weather; on moonlight nights nearer than on dark nights; in early morning nearer or farther than at midday or evening and, when seen from a height, distant places may appear close at hand. All these factors must be taken into consideration when judging of distance and much practice under varying conditions is necessary before a person can hope to guess a distance within many miles under all conditions.

It may seem a matter of little importance to be able to judge distances correctly, but in reality it is a very important branch of woodcraft. If you know a certain locality is a definite distance away you must be able to judge distances in order to know when you reach the desired spot, or again, you may often see a hill, mountain, lake or river which you wish to reach and unless you can judge of its distance, as well as bear in mind its direction while travelling towards it, you will not know how much time will be required to reach it or how far or in what direction to travel to it.

In such cases the ability to judge direction and distance, and to follow the route in mind unerringly, is of great importance, for the object you seek may be invisible or hidden from sight as you proceed towards it, and unless your mind is trained to woodcraft you may miss the desired spot or be obliged to wander about and do a lot of unnecessary travelling before you find it.

Still another matter which should be given attention is a knowledge of how to measure the height of objects, the elevation of land above water, or the height of a hill above level country, the distance across ravines, lakes or streams, etc., and to do this with real accuracy, which is a very simple matter once you know how.

I have already mentioned the compass and while nearly every one has some idea of the use of a compass and its various points few persons can name more than the eight cardinal points or can lay a course or route by compass and follow it. Under ordinary conditions the fact that a place was north, east, south, west or northeast, southeast, etc., might be sufficient; but if one is following a trail through the woods, across a plain or prairie, or over a lake or large body of water, the

difference of a point or two in the compass bearings might cause you to miss your destination completely.

On short distances such a slight variation might
make no difference, but on a tramp or voyage of
twenty-five miles or more the deviation of a quar-
ter point from the exact bearings would make a
vast difference at the end of the trip. This is
easily understood when you stop to realise that
two straight lines, drawn. from the centre of a
circle outward, always form an angle and that
the two sides of this angle separate more and more
the further they are extended, so the greater the
distance to be travelled, the more careful you must
be to lay and follow your course by compass.
Hence, when travelling with a compass as a guide,
you must refer to the instrument frequently and
must correct your course each time and unless you
take care you may go astray in doing this. The
best plan is to make a sketch or plan of the pro-
posed route, with starting and objective points
indicated, and with a straight line connecting the
two and laid down accurately with the compass
bearings. Then, by frequently comparing your
plan with your compass as you proceed, judging
the distances travelled and noting each deviation
or alteration in your course on the sketch, you can
reach the desired spot with accuracy. This is
exactly what a sailor does when navigating by
dead reckoning. Of course the necessity of this
procedure is evident if there are obstacles or ob-
structions in your way while, if crossing a lake or

level land where a straight course may be followed, it is scarcely necessary. Thus, if you find your objective point is northeast of your starting point you may be obliged to travel southeast in order to go around some swamp, cliff, pond or other obstruction and unless you can judge the distance you travel southeast and jot this and the direction you have travelled on your sketch map you will find it extremely difficult to get back on your original course. This is more readily understood by referring to *Fig. 29*, which shows a rough sketch of a route from a camp site by a lake to a mountain pass. Although the pass lies due northeast from the camp, yet the route travelled was so circuitous and indirect that the traveller moved in nearly every direction, even going southwest at times, in traversing the course, and if he had depended entirely upon his sense of direction, or upon an occasional glance at his compass, he would have gone hopelessly astray as shown by the dotted line, which indicates the course he would have followed had he always moved in a northeasterly direction each time he referred to his compass, or if he had failed to record his movements on the map. But don't expect your compass to "show you the way." It is a very useful instrument if understood and properly used, but it possesses no supernatural powers and its value depends upon your own common sense and knowledge; without this a compass is utterly useless. In addition to the compass there are many other ways of determin-

ing one's position or of following a fairly direct line. Thus the North or Pole Star is an absolutely reliable guide and every person who spends any time in the woods should be able to recognise and locate the Pole Star. This is easily done by finding the constellation known as the Great Bear or Great Dipper in the northern sky. Then, by running an imaginary line from the two outer stars of the Dipper,—the upper most of which forms the "lip" of the dipper or the "breast" of the Bear—and from the bottom of the dipper or foot of the bear upward, the first bright star on this line will be the North Star. As the dipper rotates around the Pole Star the constellation will sometimes be above and sometimes below or at one side of the north star; but if the imaginary line is run up from the bottom across the breast of the bear or lip of the dipper the North Star may always be located as shown in *Fig. 30*, provided of course the night is clear.

I have already mentioned the importance of being able to gauge distance accurately. To measure long distances the easiest method is to pace over them and with a little practice and by measuring the length of your strides you can learn to pace a distance of several hundred yards quite accurately. An ordinary man's pace is about three feet or a yard on smooth level ground, but in hilly or broken country, on soft ground, or in the woods, the length of a pace must of necessity vary and only by repeatedly pacing or walking over various kinds of ground and averaging the length of your strides can you expect to obtain a fair idea of distances travelled in this manner.

There is a little instrument known as the pedometer which will give you a very good idea of distances walked and every camper should carry one. But as this instrument is simply a device for recording and adding up your steps it must be adjusted to suit your stride or you must correct and check up results by experiment and as it records *every* step, whether short or long, you must test the pedometer by travelling known distances over various kinds of country and then adding or subtracting a definite percentage from the readings of the instrument when you use it.

For short distances, and to determine the length or height of various objects, there are much more simple and accurate means of measurement and every camper and woodsman should know how to measure the width of streams or gorges, the height of trees and the levels of hills or other heights without the aid of surveying instruments or complex mathematics.

To determine the height of an object is perhaps more simple than to measure a distance and may be accomplished as follows:

Suppose, for example, you wish to measure the height of a large tree. First place a stick or pole upright in the ground so that a definite height, say 6 feet, is above the surface of the earth, *Fig. 31 A-B.*

Then place your face close to the surface of the ground and sight across the top of the pole to the top of the tree and move further away or nearer, until the top of the pole comes exactly in line with the top of the tree as shown at C-E and measure the distance from your eye to the base of the pole, C-B, and from base of tree to your eye C-D. If you find the distance from pole to eye to be ten feet and from base of tree to eye 100 feet then, by the simple sum in ratio of 10: 6:: 100: X, you obtain the result 60 feet as the correct height of the tree.

To determine the distance of an object from the observer, or the width of a stream, pond, ravine or other space, is equally simple.

First, select some prominent landmark such as a tree, rock or building, or erect a pole on the further side of the stream, and use this as a sight

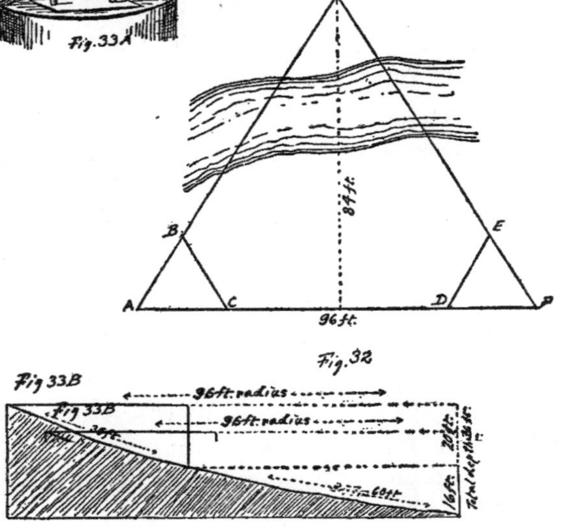

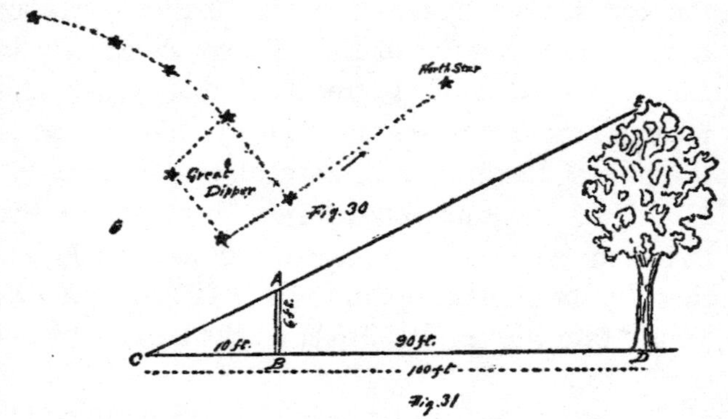

(*Fig. 32 X*). Next make a small equilateral triangle by placing three straight sticks of equal length upon the ground and in such a position that by sighting along one of the sides the corners A, B will come in line with X. Mark the three angles, A, B, C, with small stones or short sticks pushed into the earth and walk along in line with the marks A, C, until the triangle, when placed upon the ground, will have the angles E, F in line with X and the side D, F will come in line with the marks A, C. Then, by measuring the distance from A to F, you can learn the distance from G to X, for this is always ⅞ of the distance from A to F. Thus, if from A to F is 96 feet, you may be sure that from G to X is 84 feet.

Finally there is the matter of levelling, or in other words, determining the depth of a depression or the height of a hill. This is easily accomplished if you have a pail or bucket, a knife and a tape or rule for measuring. Suppose there is a shallow hollow whose depth you wish to learn.

Cut a thin flat piece of wood a little shorter than the diameter of the bucket and in each end insert a little mast or post, the two being of exactly the same height (*Fig. 33 A*). Now fill the bucket with water and secure a straight sapling or pole. Mark off spaces of a foot apart on the pole for ten feet or so and make each mark easily visible by cutting away some of the bark or attaching short cross pieces. Place the marked pole upright in the ground at the bottom of the depression, and place the pail upon the edge of the depression with the board and its two little masts towards the pole and, if the hollow is not deeper than the height of your pole, you will be able to note the foot mark which comes in line with the tops of the masts. By deducting the distance from the bottom of the pail to the tops of the masts from the mark upon the pole you will know the depth of the hollow. If, on the other hand, the hole is deeper than the height of your pole, you will have to use a longer rod or else move the rod towards the pail until your sights come in line with the marks upon the rod. Then measure the distance from the pail to the rod, set the pail where the pole was before, move the pole further into the hollow and again sight across the masts. By doing this several times and measuring the distances from pail to rod each time and adding the total heights obtained, you will not only be able to determine the depth of the depression but will be able also to make a sectional diagram of the hollow. Moreover, by this method, you can learn where the lowest part of the depression is situated, for as soon as the sights show the depth is becoming less you can be sure that the greatest depression is passed. This is more readily understood by referring to *Fig. 33 B,* which shows a sectional sketch of a hollow made by the methods described. This is also an excellent way for finding whether apparently level land rises or falls and also the height of land above water, as well as the height of a hill, for by placing the pail on the hilltop and treating the slopes like the sides of the depression an accurate outline of the hill and its height can be obtained.

By combining the use of the compass, the pedometer or paces, the use of triangulation for determining heights and distances and the simple bucket level a very accurate map of any locality may be made and you will find that in many cases such a sketch map, although made without the aid of instruments, is very useful and valuable.

CHAPTER V

EMERGENCY HINTS

Accidents, Drowning. First Aid. Bandaging. Poisons
and antidotes. Insect and snake bites.

EVERY camper should be fully prepared for any emergency, for no matter how careful you may be, how skilled you may be in woodcraft, or how experienced you are in camping, accidents *will* happen and emergencies may arise at any time.

The upsetting of a boat or canoe; a fire or a thunder storm; a high wind; a prowling wild animal; or some other cause, may bring injuries, illness or death, while a soft spot in the earth, a fallen tree, a rotten log or a slippery rock, may result in sprains, dislocations or fractures. More remote than such things is the danger of snake bites, but the stings of many insects are fully as dangerous and far more troublesome. In addition to all these, there is the ever present menace of a glancing axe or slipping knife and, wherever there is water, there is the risk of some one being drowned.

To safeguard yourself and friends against serious or fatal results from such accidents you should learn how to render first aid, how to resuscitate the drowned, how to cure snake and insect bites, and how to care for fractures, disloca-

tions, cuts or serious injuries of any kind until
the patient can be taken to a hospital or medical
aid can be summoned.

One of the first and most important things to
learn in rendering first aid is the proper way to
put on a bandage. Any strip of cloth, a napkin,
towel, handkerchief, or a piece torn from a gar-
ment, may be used as a bandage in an emergency, but oftentimes such extemporised bandages
are far from clean, and they are never sterilised
or antiseptic and, as a result, they may cause inflammation, or even blood poisoning. It is far
better always to be provided with regular surgeons' bandages of sterilised antiseptic gauze of
assorted widths. The ideal bandage for extensive
or serious injuries is, however, the *Esmach* triangular bandage, for this is far easier to apply
than any other form. Any one can make a bandage of this sort by cutting a piece of cloth 40
inches square into two triangular halves, but the
prepared bandage is better and if a home-made
bandage is used it should be scrupulously clean
and should be disinfected with carbolic acid, or
some similar solution, and kept hermetically
sealed until wanted for use.

The regulation bandages, as furnished to the
army and navy, have printed directions with dia-
grams illustrating their use, stamped in indelible
ink and every camper should study these until he
has memorised the methods of using the bandages
for any wound or injury that may occur. These
triangular bandages may be used open for injuries

to the head, etc., or they may be folded to use as slings or rolled, folded and arranged to suit the needs of any part of the limbs or body requiring a bandage. When thus folded the bandage is of the greatest value in holding splints or dressings in place, for slings, for tourniquets, etc.

When fastening a bandage of any sort, either use a strong safety pin, or else tear down the ends a short distance and tie the strips with square or reef knots. Never use a bow knot, slip-knot or "granny." Such knots are liable to loosen or become unfastened accidentally.

In making a sling, fold the bandage or a large piece of strong cloth as in *Fig. 1.* Place one end over the shoulder of the injured side and let the free end hang down. Then carefully bend the arm at right angles at the elbow,—with the thumb uppermost,—draw the loose end of the sling up outside of the arm and over the opposite shoulder and fasten it to the first end (*Fig. 2 A*).

Never attempt to bend an injured arm and place it in a sling already tied. If a broad sling is required, as in the case of an injury to the upper arm, make the cloth wide enough to cover the forearm and more. Then place the end of sling across the shoulder opposite the injury, bend the injured arm carefully at elbow, place it across breast with palm of hand inward and thumb up, bring the end of sling up across forearm, pass it over shoulder on the injured side and fasten ends securely behind the neck. Then draw the point of the bandage forward over the elbow and pin it in place. This is the sort of sling which should be used for any injury to the upper arm, a broken collar bone, a dislocated elbow or shoulder or a sprained wrist or elbow (*Fig. 2 B*).

Injuries to the head are often very difficult to bandage properly, but with a large triangular bandage there should be little trouble. If the wound is large, the bandage should be used open and not folded, but one edge should be turned on itself to form a thick edge or hem. Place the bandage with the centre of this folded edge over forehead, and with the edge in line with the eyebrows, so that the point of the bandage hangs over the back of the neck. Then gather both ends around the head above the ears with the point underneath. Cross the ends and bring them around to the front of head and tie securely over the forehead. Then pull the point down so the whole fits the head like a cap and turn the point up over the ends and pin it in position as shown in *Fig. 3*.

For small wounds or minor injuries to the head, ears or eyes, the bandage should be folded as shown in *Fig. 1*, and should be applied as illustrated in *Fig. 4*. For shoulder wounds, place the border of the bandage downwards over the middle of arm with the point on the upper surface of the shoulder, or beside the neck, and bring the two ends around the arm, crossing them on the inside and tying on the outer side. Then bend the forearm at elbow and place it in a sling as already described. Finally, draw the point of the bandage under and around the sling where it passes around the neck on the injured side and pin in position as shown in *Fig. 5.*

Wounds or any injuries to the hands are comparatively easy to dress or bandage and for such purposes there are two good ways of using the tri-

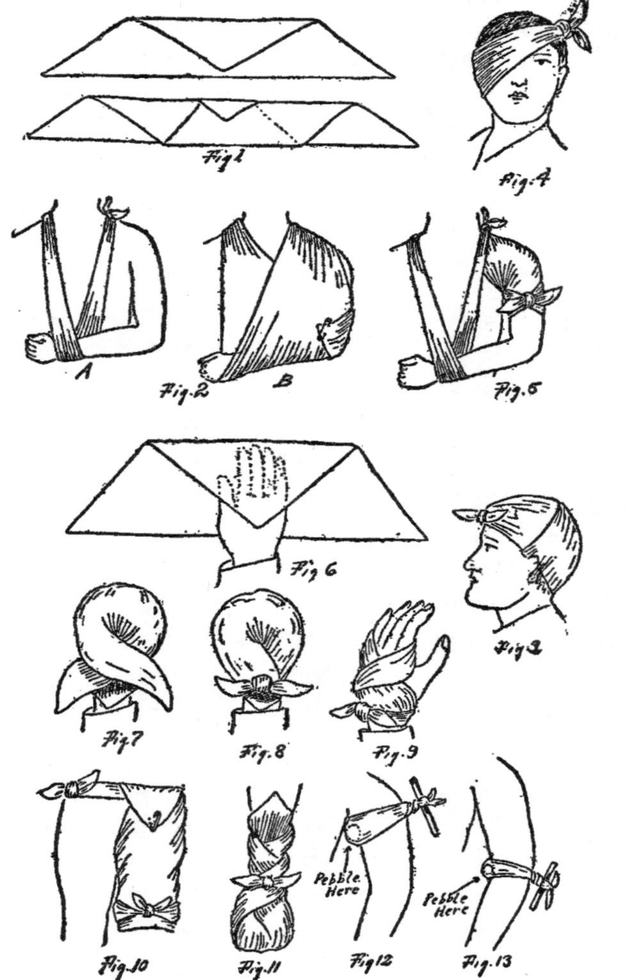

angular bandage,—whether the entire hand is to be covered or whether only a portion requires bandaging. For a bandage for the entire hand, the triangular cloth should be spread out, the hand placed palm down upon it, with the fingers toward the point of the triangle, and with the wrist in the centre of the lower border. Then turn the point over, back and down over the wrist (*Fig. 6*), and bring the ends around the wrist and over the point (*Fig. 7*). Cross the ends, bring them back and tie over the point and finally draw the point up so that the bandage fits the hand snugly (*Fig. 8*).

Where it is only required to cover the fingers, or a portion of the hand, fold the bandage to the right width and place the centre over the wound with a poultice, compress or dressing beneath it; bring the ends around, cross them obliquely, bring them around the wrist and tie. *Fig. 9.*

Where the hip or thigh is injured, two bandages are used, one of which is applied in a similar manner as described for the shoulder. First fold one bandage until narrow and use this like a belt around the waist, with the knot on the side opposite to the injury. Then place the triangular bandage over the wounded hip, with the lower edge on the middle of the thigh, and with the point up, pass the ends around thigh and cross and tie them on the outside. Finally, pass the point under the girdle, bring it down and secure with a pin. *Fig. 10.*

In case the leg is injured below the hip and

above the foot the bandage is folded and used by passing around the limb several times and is then tied on the side opposite to the injury.

For bandaging the foot the triangle should be opened out, and the foot rested upon it, with the toes towards the point. The point should then be carried over the instep, both ends are brought forward and over the point, crossing behind and catching the lower border of the bandage, and are then brought forward again and tied in front of the ankle. The point is then brought down over the knot and pinned (*Fig. 11*). Very often a wound may bleed so freely that a *tourniquet* is required to prevent the patient from bleeding to death. A tourniquet is merely a cord, band, or strip of cloth, bound tightly around a limb to stop the flow of blood by compressing the veins or arteries, and it should always be applied above the wound and at some spot where the arteries are near the surface. Such places are the knee, the armpit, above the elbow, the wrist, the side of the neck and the groin. Usually a folded rag or handkerchief placed around a limb, and twisted tightly by means of a stick or rod, will serve every purpose, but in severe cases a pebble, lump of clay, wad of cloth or leaves, a bit of wood or even a nut should be inserted under the tourniquet in order to press upon the arteries directly. Two methods of applying tourniquets are illustrated in *Figs. 12* and *13*. The former showing how to apply a tourniquet for a wound above the elbow and the other how to use one for a wound below the elbow.

In case a *cut* or *injury* is received in the *arm* or *hand* the wounded man should hold the limb above the head as this will decrease the flow of blood until a tourniquet is applied. So, too, in case a leg or foot is injured the limb should be kept higher than the head if possible and should always be elevated until a tourniquet is applied.

Fractured bones should be bound with splints, which are light strong pieces of stick or wood, fastened in place by binding with a rag, bandage, cord or handkerchief.

Sprains should be attended to at once as otherwise very serious results may follow. Raise the injured limb, support it carefully, don't move the joint, and apply luke warm lotions or poultices. As soon as inflammation ceases apply liniments, spray parts alternately with lukewarm and cold water, or apply hot and cold compresses in turn, and bandage tightly.

Treat dislocations in the same way until medical aid can be secured, for unless you are skilled you will do more harm than good by attempting to pull a dislocated joint into place. However, if there must be much delay in securing a doctor you may be obliged to pull the joint into position. Then bandage with compresses as for a sprain until inflammation ceases.

Burns and *scalds* should be kept covered from the air and for this purpose flour and oil, grease and flour, limewater and oil, cooking soda and oil or grease, and similar compounds, should be applied. *Never* break the blister caused by a burn or scald and keep them well covered with soft lint held in place by a bandage.

Severe bruises or *contusions* are best treated by applying hot water compresses until inflammation subsides, after which they may be poulticed with alcohol, vinegar and water, arnica or any good liniment.

Shocks of any kind in which the patient faints or becomes helpless, pale or weak, should be treated by placing the patient on his back with head and shoulders slightly raised and clothing loosened about neck and waist. Give brandy and water, whisky and water, or aromatic spirits of ammonia and water, every two minutes in small doses. Large doses of stimulants should *never* be given under such conditions. Apply warm or hot applicants to limbs and pit of stomach, rub limbs briskly and wrap patient in warm blankets. As soon as the patient recovers full consciousness give strong hot soup or coffee.

Sunstroke is quite a different matter from ordinary shock or fainting spells. First take patient into the shade and place in a recumbent attitude with elevated head and shoulders. Loosen clothes about neck and body and apply ice, cold wet cloths or ice water to head and nape of neck and change frequently. Drench head, spine and chest with cold water, pouring it on from a height of two feet or more. Fan patient briskly and apply mustard to limbs and sides and administer small doses of stimulants.

If a person is overcome with gas, charcoal fumes, smoke or, is in other words, *asphyxiated,* the face becomes livid and the condition may easily be mistaken for actual death. The first thing to do under such conditions is to place the patient with head raised where there is an abundance of fresh clear air. Remove the clothing and drench body with cold water. Then apply fumes of ammonia or smelling salts to nostrils; sponge body and face with vinegar and water and rub briskly. In severe cases you may be obliged to resort to artificial respiration as directed for reviving the apparently drowned.

Frostbites and *frozen fingers, toes, ears* or *limbs* are common in the North during winter, and every camper should know how to treat such cases. Use friction on the affected parts; first rubbing with snow and then with cold water, until the frost is removed, which will be indicated by the dead-white frozen flesh resuming its pink tint and by returning sensation. As soon as this occurs, administer brandy or whiskey and water in small quantities and keep patient in motion and exercising the parts which have been frozen. If the patient is insensible from exposure, or is apparently dead, the body should be stripped, covered with snow or ice, and placed in cold water. When the body is thawed out, place it in a dry, but cold, bed and rub hard under cover. Don't be discouraged, but continue using friction for hours. If signs of life appear, give small injections of camphor and water or place a few drops of strong spirits on the tongue. Then rub body with spirits and water, gradually increasing the spirits until clear spirits are used. Then give hot coffee, hot tea, or brandy and water.

Wherever there is a lake, pond, stream or salt water there is always the danger of drowning, for even the best swimmer may be overcome by cramps, cold or exhaustion, or in an upset of a canoe or boat, some blow or injury may be received by which the inmates lose consciousness and are unable to save themselves.

Every one, whether a camper or not, should know how to revive, or, at least, try to revive, the apparently drowned, for it is knowledge which will never come amiss and may save valuable lives at any time.

The first thing to be done,—unless the weather is very severe and there is danger of freezing,—is to commence your efforts as near the spot where the body is taken from the water as is possible, and not, as is sometimes done, wait until the victim has been carried to some house or other distant spot. Expose the face to a free current of air at once, wipe the mouth and nose dry, loosen or strip off garments from chest and waist, and give two or three quick, resounding slaps with the open hand on stomach and chest. If the patient has lost consciousness for only a few minutes, this will often be sufficient to revive him. If, however, there is no sign of his coming to, proceed as follows:

If jaws are clenched, separate them and keep mouth open by a bit of wood or cork between

the teeth, and if you cannot pry jaws apart, don't
hesitate to knock out a few front teeth to accomplish your purpose, for teeth do not count, as com-
pared to life.   Turn the patient on his face, with
a bundle of clothes, a log, barrel, timber or a person's knee beneath his stomach, and press steadily
and heavily upon the back for half a minute,
or as long as liquids or water flow from the
mouth.

Then clear mouth and throat of mucus by a
rag or handkerchief wrapped around your finger,
and turn the body on its back, with a roll of clothing or some other object underneath, so as to raise
the stomach slightly.   If there is another person
present, have him hold the tip of the patient's
tongue out of one corner of the mouth, and, with
his other hand, let him grasp both the patient's
wrists and keep the arms stretched above the
head.

If alone, try to tie the loose-hanging tongue of
your patient with the tip of your handkerchief, or
any other cord or rag, so it will not fall back and
close the windpipe.   Kneel astride the body,
or beside it, and place your hands on the lower
part of the chest, with the balls of your thumbs
resting on either side of the pit of stomach, and
your fingers resting between the short ribs, so as
to grasp the waist.   Then, using your knees as a
pivot, throw your weight forward on your hands,
at the same time squeezing the waist as if you
intended to force the contents of the chest up
through the mouth.   Deepen the pressure steadily
while you count slowly one, two, three, and then

let go suddenly with a final push which will spring you back to your kneeling position. Remain stationary while again counting one, two, three, and then repeat the operation as before, but gradually increasing the speed from four or five to fifteen times a minute, and keep up the bellows-like movements with as near the same regularity as occurs in the natural motion of breathing as is possible.

If, at the end of three or four minutes, breathing does not commence, then, without ceasing the movements, turn the patient on his stomach, rolling the body in the opposite direction from that in which it was first turned, and continue artificial respiration for from one to four hours, or until the patient breathes or all hope is abandoned.

Even after breathing commences, it is best to continue artificial motion for a few minutes. Then rub and dry with all the friction at your command, and, for that matter, if there is some one to help, you should have kept him rubbing the patient's limbs and body from the first.

Rub the limbs upward towards the body, and continue until long after natural respiration is restored. Then apply hot flannels to stomach and armpits, and use hot water bottles, heated bricks, and every other means to maintain artificial heat until the patient has regained vitality.

When breathing is fully restored, the patient should be placed in a warm bed with abundance of fresh air, and should be given perfect rest and allowed to sleep as long as possible. During the first hour after the patient is revived, a little brandy and water, or other stimulants, should be administered every ten or fifteen minutes.

The only real danger, after respiration is restored, is in the liability of pneumonia or congestion of the lungs, and the patient should be carefully watched and, in case any difficulty in breathing develops, apply a mustard plaster on chest and assist with artificial respiration.

Never attempt to keep a resuscitated person from sleeping, for perfect rest is imperative and death may result if at least 48 hours' rest is not maintained.

Finally, let me caution you *never* to abandon hope in trying to revive a drowned person unless he has been under water over thirty minutes, or until you are convinced there is no possible hope. Four hours' work is sometimes required to revive drowned persons, and cases are on record where people who have been under water for 25 minutes have been revived and have recovered with no ill effects. No amount of work is too great when a human life is at stake, and it often happens that efforts are abandoned after a few minutes, when, by continuing, the life of the patient might be saved. The only way of knowing if all hope must be given up, is by some test,—such as burning the skin, to see if a blister forms, by cutting a small vein, to see if blood flows, etc., and even these tests often fail. But if, after three or four hours steady work, there is no sign of returning breath, it is pretty conclusive evidence that resuscitation is impossible.

Don't imagine that you can commence to revive a drowned person and can do it properly after reading a description. Get some friend to let you practise on him, and let him practise on you, until you master each motion and operation perfectly, or, better still, ask some life guard or other expert to teach you the necessary motions, until you are proficient.

In case of a *snake bite,* the best method to follow is to bind a tourniquet above the wound, make an incision at the spot where the fangs entered, suck the wound sharply, and rub in crystals of permanganate of potash, which should always be part of your equipment in a country where venomous snakes occur. After this is done, bandage the wound with a compress of cold water, flaxseed meal or raw steak, meat, or even bread dough, and keep the wound open until inflammation and swelling cease. Also give frequent *small* doses of brandy or whiskey and *keep patient moving.* Large doses of liquor only add to the effects of the poison and many a man, bitten by a snake, has succumbed to the whiskey and not to the snake poison. Also, give strong hot coffee until drowsiness and weakness have passed off. After swelling and inflammation have disappeared from the bite and its vicinity, apply healing ointments and disinfectants to the wound, exactly as for any other cut.

For relieving the pain or itching of insect bites or stings, ammonia is excellent, but the best remedy of all is 5% formaline solution. This smarts outrageously for a few moments, but it relieves and cures, which is the main thing. Moreover, formaline of this strength is a powerful germicide and disinfectant, and I have used it with great success on boils, sores, ulcers, bites, cuts and other wounds. Always carry some formaline with you and you'll find it useful in a hundred ways.

Iodine, too, is excellent for insect bites, as well as for boils, bruises, small cuts and sores, while permanganate of potash in solution is very good for insect bites which have become inflamed and swollen.

In the woods, there is not much danger of poisoning from acids, etc., but there is always the danger of poisoning by *poisonous plants.* For the latter, use a weak solution of creosote or formaline; paint with iodine or apply some healing ointment, such as mercurial or zinc ointment, if the poisoned area is extensive and raw. The main thing to be avoided is breaking the tiny blisters which form and thus spreading the poison, and any ointment or dressing which will dry up the blisters and protect the skin is excellent. Cooking soda is also good. For other poisons, use the following antidotes.

First of all administer the antidote and then produce vomiting. It's a mistake to try to produce vomiting first, for the patient may succumb to the effects of the poison while you are doing this, or the poison may paralyse the stomach or irritate it until vomiting is impossible. The best emetic is mustard and water in the proportion of a tablespoon of mustard in a cup of water. A spoonful or two of salt in water is good, and if none of these are available thrust a finger down the throat or tickle the palate with a feather or straw. As soon as vomiting has taken place, give plentifully of warm water, soap and water or oil, to keep up the nausea until all the contents are expelled from the stomach.

For Strong Acids.—Give common chalk; oil; soap suds; soda, or any common harmless alkali.

For Arsenic, Paris Green and Similar Arsenical Compounds.—Magnesia; milk; raw eggs; powdered charcoal; oil, or limewater.

For Prussic Acid.—Cold affusion; brandy and ammonia, or powerful heart stimulants of any sort.

For Opium, Morphine, Cocaine, etc.—Keep patient moving; give strong coffee; slap with hands or switches; sting with nettles; rub with mustard, etc.

Almost as important as knowing how to care for sick or injured persons is the knowledge of how to carry or move them. There are many ways of doing this, depending largely upon the extent or seriousness of the injuries, the size or weight of the victim, the distance he is to be carried, and the conveniences at hand.

In the first place, *never* carry a patient face down by arms and legs.

Never carry an injured person on a loose blanket, clothing, curtain or similar object, as a corner may slip or the fabric may tear and drop the patient.

Never carry a patient in a stretcher upon one's shoulders, but always by the hands or straps over shoulders.

In using a litter or stretcher, care should be taken to have it strong enough to bear the patient's weight safely. A door, shutter, blind or hammock may be used as a stretcher, or one may be improvised from a strong overcoat by turning sleeves inside out, buttoning the coat over the sleeves, and passing a pole through each sleeve. In the woods, a stretcher may easily be made by using branches tied or lashed together with vines, roots, bark or twisted handkerchiefs and then covered with branches, leaves, grass or ferns. When a litter is carried by two persons, they should be careful not to keep in step, but the one in front should start with the right foot and the rear bearer with the left foot. In case the two are of unequal height, the taller should be at the patient's head. Carry the patient feet first, except in going up stairs or ascending a steep hill, when the head should go first. In case of a broken or injured thigh or leg, this rule should be reversed, for the object is to prevent an undue flow of blood to the injured part, which should, therefore, be kept higher than the rest of the body.

If one is alone with an injured comrade or a stretcher is not available, there are several methods of carrying the patient with little pain and with slight effort on his part. If the victim is conscious and is able to move, he should place one arm over your shoulder, so that his armpit rests on your shoulder, with the arm itself around your neck and over the opposite shoulder. Then, with your hand on that side, grasp his wrist and pass your other arm around his waist, as shown in *Fig. 14.* Another method is to carry the injured person "Pick-a-Back." This is a good method for children or people of light weight. Still another way, when there are two or more persons present, is to carry the injured man by the "four-handed chair" method, so well known to school children, or the "fore and aft" carry may be used, as shown in *Fig. 15.* To pick up patient by this method, one person should stand at the head and pass his arms beneath the back, under the arm-pits, and lock fingers over chest, while the bearer at the feet should pass one hand around each knee and carry a leg under each arm, as shown.

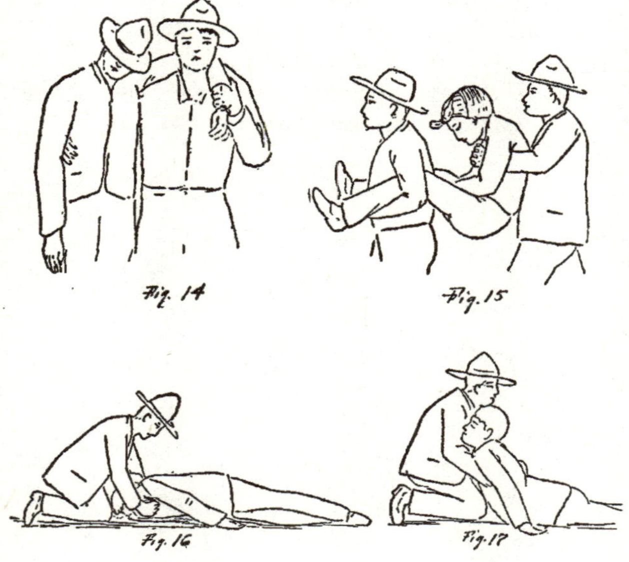

Fig. 14   Fig. 15

Fig. 16   Fig. 17

People who are unconscious from smoke, gas, drowning, etc., and who have no wounds which would be opened, or bones broken, to be made worse by rough handling, may be carried across one's shoulders, thus leaving one hand free. There are several different ways of getting a patient onto one's shoulders and while is seems like a difficult matter at first, once the knack is acquired and the trick learned, you will find it easy to pick up and carry a person who weighs more than yourself. The best of these methods for *shouldering* a body is that known as the *fireman's lift* and is accomplished as follows:

First,—Kneel on both knees at the patient's head, facing him; and turn him face down and straighten his arms at sides. *Fig. 16.*

Second,—Pass hands under his body, grasp him under armpits, raise the body as high as possible while still kneeling and let it rest on your knees. *Fig. 17.*

Third,—Pass both arms around waist of patient and lift him to an upright position with the body towards your right shoulder and thus rise. *Fig. 18.*

Fourth,—Seize the patient's right hand in your left hand
and throw his right arm around your neck. Stoop
down and place your head beneath his body and at
the same time pass your right arm around his legs,
thus bringing his weight on the centre of your back.
Fig. 22.

Fifth,—Seize his right hand or wrist with your right hand,
balance his body carefully on your shoulders and
stand erect. *Fig. 20.*

All of these various matters should be practised
from time to time, and it is a splendid idea to
have regular practice drills at stated times while
camping out. The more familiar you become
with each motion, action and treatment, the better fitted will you be to cope with any emergency
which may arise, and, moreover, you will not be so
liable to lose your head or get frightened at the
sight of bleeding wounds or broken bones. But
no matter how well trained you may be in first
aid, how much self-control you may have, or how
skilled you are in simple medicine or surgery,
don't fail to secure competent medical or surgical
aid at the earliest moment, if an injury or illness
gives the least sign of being serious. An ounce
of prevention is worth tons of cure in the woods.

THE END